Basics of Banking for Freshers

Bijoy Bhusan Bhattacharyya

M.A. (Economics), LL.B.
Dean (Banking),
Welingkar Institute of
Management Development
& Research, Mumbai.

Himalaya Publishing House

MUMBAI • NEW DELHI • NAGPUR • BENGALURU • HYDERABAD • CHENNAI • PUNE • LUCKNOW • AHMEDABAD • ERNAKULAM • BHUBANESWAR • INDORE • KOLKATA • GUWAHATI

First Edition : 2014

Published by : Mrs. Meena Pandey for **Himalaya Publishing House Pvt. Ltd.,** "Ramdoot", Dr. Bhalerao Marg, Girgaon, Mumbai - 400 004. Phone: 022-23860170/23863863, Fax: 022-23877178 **E-mail: himpub@vsnl.com; Website: www.himpub.com**

Branch Offices :

New Delhi : "Pooja Apartments", 4-B, Murari Lal Street, Ansari Road, Darya Ganj, New Delhi - 110 002. Phone: 011-23270392, 23278631; Fax: 011-23256286

Nagpur : Kundanlal Chandak Industrial Estate, Ghat Road, Nagpur - 440 018. Phone: 0712-2738731, 3296733; Telefax: 0712-2721216

Bengaluru : No. 16/1 (Old 12/1), 1st Floor, Next to Hotel Highlands, Madhava Nagar, Race Course Road, Bengaluru - 560 001. Phone: 080-22286611, 22385461, 4113 8821, 22281541

Hyderabad : No. 3-4-184, Lingampally, Besides Raghavendra Swamy Matham, Kachiguda, Hyderabad - 500 027. Phone: 040-27560041, 7550139

Chennai : 8/2 Madley 2nd street, T. Nagar, Chennai - 600 017. Mobile: 09320490962

Pune : First Floor, "Laksha" Apartment, No. 527, Mehunpura Shaniwarpeth (Near Prabhat Theatre), Pune - 411 030. Phone: 020-24 496323/24496333; Mobile: 09370579333

Lucknow : House No 731, Shekhupura Colony, Near B.D. Convent School, Aliganj, Lucknow - 226 022. Phone: 0522-4012353; Mobile: 09307501549

Ahmedabad : 114, "SHAIL", 1st Floor, Opp. Madhu Sudan House, C.G. Road, Navrang Pura, Ahmedabad - 380 009. Phone: 079-26560126; Mobile: 09377088847

Ernakulam : 39/104 A, Lakshmi Apartment, Karikkamuri Cross Rd., Ernakulam, Cochin - 622011, Kerala. Phone: 0484-2378012, 2378016; Mobile: 09387122121

Bhubaneswar : 5 Station Square, Bhubaneswar - 751 001 (Odisha). Phone: 0674-2532129, Mobile: 09338746007

Indore : Kesardeep Avenue Extension, 73, Narayan Bagh, Flat No. 302, IIIrd Floor, Near Humpty Dumpty School, Indore - 452 007 (M.P.). Mobile: 09303399304

Kolkata : 108/4, Beliaghata Main Road, Near ID Hospital, Opp. SBI Bank, Kolkata - 700 010, Phone: 033-32449649, Mobile: 7439040301

Guwahati : House No. 15, Behind Pragjyotish College, Near Sharma Printing Press, P.O. Bharalumukh, Guwahati - 781009, (Assam). Mobile: 09883055590, 08486355289, 7439040301

DTP by : **Hansa Subhedar**

Printed at : M/s Sri Sai Art Printer Hyderabad. On behalf of HPH.

Dedicated to
My Late Father
&
Mother

FOREWORD

बी. वी. उपाध्ये
महाप्रबंधक
B. V. Upadhye
General Manager

1. I take immense pleasure in writing the Foreword to the book "Basics of Banking for Freshers" authored by Prof. Bijoy Bhushan Bhattacharyya, Dean Banking, Wellingkar Institute of Management and Exer-AGM, Bank of India, who is a practicing banker for over 40 years. He has successfully worked as a Branch Manager, Zonal Manager, Administrative Office and India Based Officer (at Singapore). He had successful stints as faculty of NIBM, Pune and as Principal of BOI's Staff Training College at Bhopal.
2. With the financial sector reforms, the banking sector has undergone tremendous changes in terms of business process, market orientation and management sophistication. The need for understanding the challenges and meaningfully updating knowledge to meet the challenges requires a fundamental appreciation of various core aspects of business of banking and finance in the changing environment for all the employees of banks. This calls for excellence in performance.
3. A quick perusal of the book reveals that it is quite comprehensive, exhaustive and suitable for students of Finance. The book will be of great help to the new entrants in the banking industry, especially for their orientation to the core operational areas of banking. Prof. Bhattacharyya has taken tremendous efforts to initiate freshers in banking be it officers or clerks. It will benefit those specialist officers also who do not have operational exposure in branches.
4. The book covers Retail Banking, Corporate Loans, Priority Sector Lending, Non-performing Assets, Treasury and ALM, Foreign Exchange Basic and the latest Risk Management topics like Capital Adequacy Ratios.
5. I feel the book by Prof. Bhattacharyya will serve the purpose of reference book and a Manual of Instructions on Banking which will be quite handy for referring to the basics of any kind of banking operations.

Mumbai – 400 051
Date: 01.11.2013

(B.V. Upadhye)

प्रधान कार्यालय : स्टार हाऊस, सी-5, "जी" ब्लॉक, 4 थी मंजिल, बांद्रा-कुर्ला संकुल, बांद्रा (पूर्व), मुंबई-400 051. Website : www.bankofindia.co.in
Head Office : Star House, C-5, "G" Block, 4th Floor, Bandra-Kurla Complex, Bandra (East), Mumbai-400 051. ✆ 022 - 6668 4986 / 4730 ℻ 022 - 6668 4786
Email : HeadOffice.RM@bankofindia.co.in / Bhalchandra.Upadhye@bankofindia.co.in

PREFACE

Banking, world over, has been changing. India is no exception. Some factors of change are common all over the world, e.g., technological development, increasing globalization, deregulation and re-regulation, customer awareness and resultant expectations, competition and consequent pressure on profit margins etc. Some factors, however, are country-specific, e.g., in case of India, nationalization of banks, thrust on financial inclusion, difficulties of raising additional capital etc. History has shown that Indian Banking, has been able to withstand various changes in the economic environment successfully, the last being global financial crisis. But past success is not a source of comfort for future, particularly in the field of finance and banking.

Today, every bank employee needs to be strong with domain knowledge. Each and every young banker who is joining the industry needs to be fundamentally strong on Basics of Banking. Once basics are clear, subsequent add-ons will be meaningful and effective. With this end in view, ***'Basics of Banking for Freshers'*** is written. The book covers various important areas of banking like Retail Banking, Corporate Loans, Priority Sector Lending, NPA, Treasury and ALM, Foreign Exchange and Capital Adequacy Norms all in basic and primary language so as to offer freshers an opportunity to understand the concepts through self-reading. Examples have also been given. This book is expected to be of benefit for anyone new to banking, desirous of assuming leadership positions in future and developing the skills of critical and analytical thinking in order to withstand challenges of modern banking.

Author

ACKNOWLEDGEMENTS

I specially thank my son, Manosij, for enthusing me in this work as he had been after me for years to write a book on Banking. I thank my wife, Krishna, for enquiring with me from time to time about the progress of the book. I thank Dr. Uday Salunkhe, Group Director, WE School, for providing me enough opportunities and enthusiasm in creative work. I thank Mrs. Anjali A. Kulkarni for her efforts not only in typing, but organizing and giving valuable suggestions from time to time.

Author

CONTENTS

DETAILED CONTENTS

Chapter 1

RETAIL BANKING

Introduction

Indian Banking has come a long way and withstood many storms both national and international. We are in the reform era for the last two decades. Presently, the banking statistics reflect the following:

Tyes of Banks	No. of Banks	No. of Branches	% Share of No. of Branches	Market Share of Assets %
Public Sector	26	67,466	83	72.8
Private Sector	20	13,452	16.6	20.2
Foreign Banks	41	323	0.4	7
Total	87	81,241	100	100

(***Source:*** Speech of Dr. D. Subbarao, at the FICCI – IBA Annual Meeting on 13/8/2013 in Mumbai)

Thus, it appears Public Sector Banks even now, occupies a pivotal position inasmuch as 73% of market share of assets and 83% of branches. In the post 1991 reform era, 12 banks have been given licence and a few more are under consideration of Reserve Bank of India and would be given shortly. These banks are likely to bring in more competition, resultant efficiency and also improved products and services.

Banking is a mix of traditional and changing concepts. Whereas acceptance of deposits and lending and investing are basic functions of banking traditionally which is known as intermediation function, changes are also taking place worldwide caused primarily by deregulation, globalization, technological advancement and competition. We have learnt over various economic crises to introduce new changes in regulatory measures over banking, non-banking and shadow banking institutions. Thus, banking industry is poised for rapid reforms and changes.

Basically, a bank would have the following five main organs and five supporting segments:

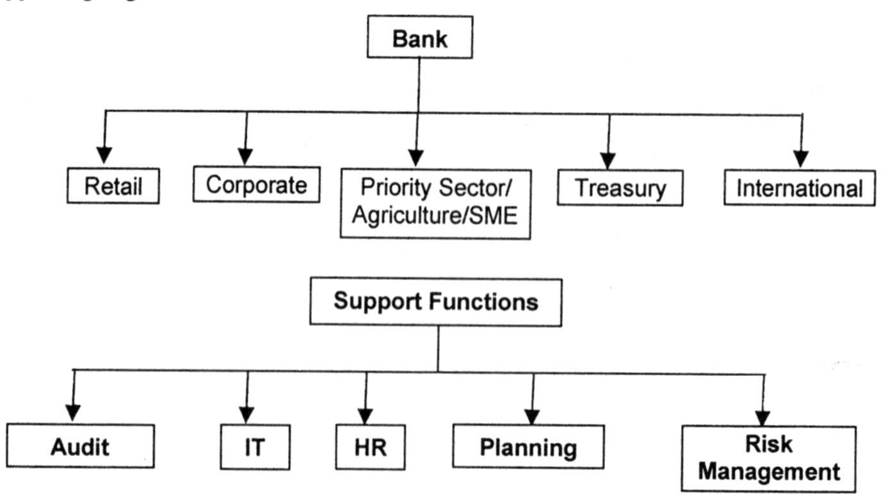

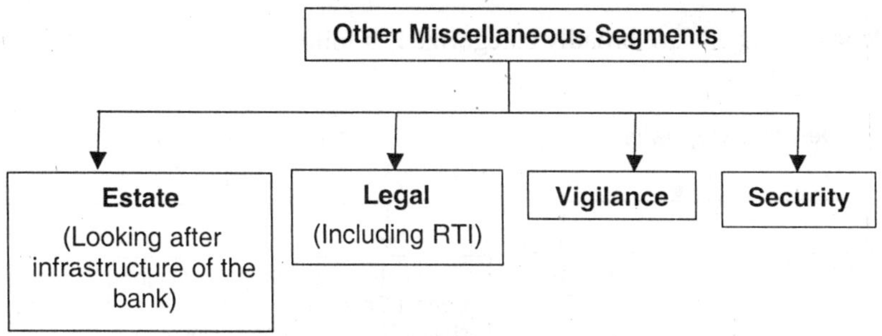

Figure 1

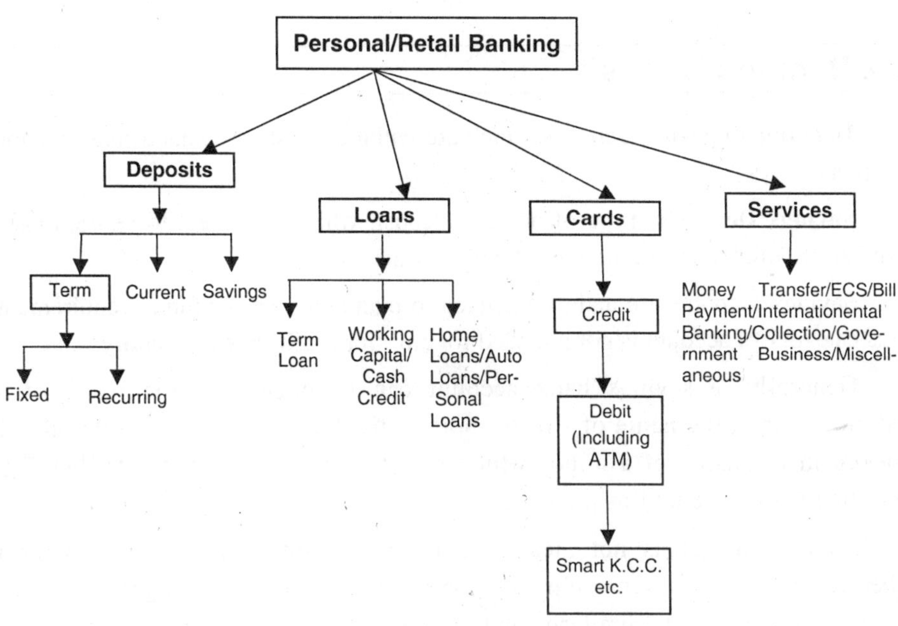

Figure 2

1.1 Retail Banking Products

Retail banking as the name suggests, refers to banking services whether on asset side (Loans) or liabilities side (Deposits) as applied to individuals and small businessmen.

As can be seen from above "Deposits" are of three categories broadly – Term, Current and Savings. Flexi Deposits, Sweep-in and Sweep-out Deposits etc. are all different variants of/combination of the above three types of deposits.

Deposit products are broadly categorized as follows:

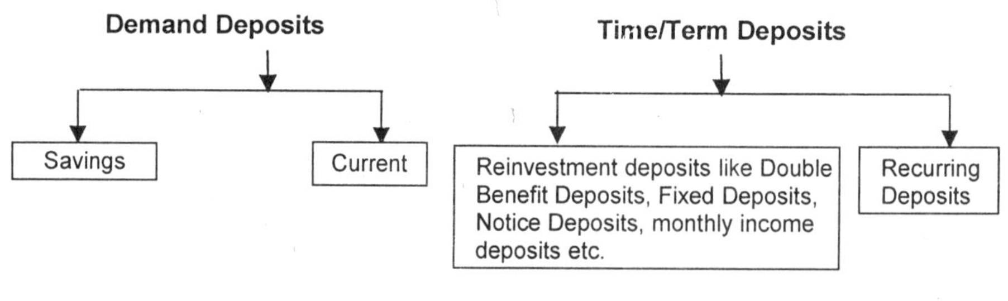

Figure 3

1.2 Demand Deposit

Demand Deposits: Deposits which are withdrawable on demand (e.g., Savings, Current).

Savings Deposits: Type of demand deposit which is subject to restrictions on number of withdrawals or amount of withdrawals.

Savings accounts are mainly intended to plan and save for future requirements. This category of account is not intended for any 'for profit' business entity.

Generally, a savings bank account can be opened in the name of an individual or in the name of two or more individuals. The account can also be opened in the name of a minor which will be operated upon by his/her legal guardian till he/she attains majority.

As this facility is not meant for business entities, no business concern whether proprietary/partnership or company/association is eligible to open savings bank account. Similarly, entities like, Government Departments, State Electricity Boards, Housing Boards, also cannot open a savings account. However, Reserve Bank permitted Public Sector Banks vide its order dated January 24,2000 to open savings bank accounts in the name of Collector/District Magistrate/District Commissioner in respect of funds selected for implementation of member of parliament Local Area Development Scheme. Banks were also permitted by Reserve Bank of India to open savings bank accounts in the name of Zilla Parishad/Gram Panchayats for placement of funds released for implementation of various rural development/welfare programmes.

Savings Bank Scheme is generally available at all the branches of banks. Minimum balance varies from bank to bank, centre to centre and with or without cheque book facility. Normally, the structure of minimum balance in public sector banks is as follows:

Centre	With Cheque Book Facility	Ordinary Account (Without Cheque Book Facility)
Metro/Urban	₹ 1,000	₹ 500
Semi-urban	₹ 1,000	₹ 500
Rural	₹ 500	₹ 250

There are charges for violating minimum balance criteria which varies from bank to bank. Private sector and Foreign Banks insist on minimum balance of ₹ 5,000 to ₹ 10,000 generally.

1.3 Opening a Saving Account

Who Can Open?

Any person who is eligible to enter into contract and complies with 'Know Your Customer' (KYC) formalities as follows:

KYC primarily involves: (1) identification of the customer and (2) proof of address. Any of the following documents is acceptable to the Bank as KYC requirement for purposes of establishment of identity and proof of address.

(a) **Valid Passport:** Contains both identity proof as well as address proof.

(b) **PAN Card/Driving Licence:** Identity proof.

(c) **Voters ID Card:** Identity proof.

(d) **Defence ID Card:** Identity proof.

(e) **Identity Card of Central/State Govt. Employees and Public Sector Undertakings:** Identity proof.

(f) **Aadhar Card:** Identity and address proof.

(g) **Utility bills:** Address proof.

This type of account can be opened in own name or in the name of two or more persons under following mode of operation:

(a) Either or Survivor

(b) Jointly or Survivor

(c) Either or the Survivors jointly

(d) 'Former or Survivor' or 'Latter or Survivor'

Account can also be opened in the single name of a minor who has completed the age of 10 years and is able to read and write. Account can be opened in the name of minor jointly with his/her guardian.

Any Club, Society, Trusts, some Government Departments/bodies, etc. can also open this Account:

1. **Pass Book:** Bank issues pass books/statements to account holders free of charge evidencing transactions in the account. If the pass book is lost or spoiled, the depositor will have to pay necessary charges for issuing duplicate pass book. The pass book should be sent to the bank periodically for updating.

2. **Withdrawals:** A person may withdraw the amount by Cash or by Cheque. Total number of withdrawals may vary between 30 and 120 per half year. Public sector banks generally restrict the cheques to be drawn about 20/25 a month.

3. **Interest rate:** Paid on half-yearly intervals and is computed on daily balance basis.

Even after liberalization and consequent deregulation, savings bank was the only deposit scheme where interest rate was regulated @ 3.5% p.a. since March 2003 usually credited to customers' account half-yearly. Savings deposit is a hybrid product because it contains features of current account (which is primarily meant for transaction purposes) and term deposit account. Savings accounts are maintained for both transactions purposes and savings for future mostly by individuals and households.

In the second quarter review of monetary policy announcement on 25/10/2011, Reserve Bank decided to deregulate the savings bank interest rate. Accordingly, it was decided that Banks were free to determine their savings bank interest rates subject, of course, to the following conditions:

(a) Each bank will have to offer an uniform interest rate on savings bank deposits upto a limit of ₹ 1 lakh – irrespective of the amount in the account within this limit.

(b) Second, for savings bank deposit over ₹ 1 lakh, a bank may provide differential rates of interest, if it so chooses, subject to the condition that banks will not discriminate in the matter of interest rate for a similar amount of deposits. This means, upto a deposit of ₹ 1 lakh, interest rate earned by depositors from a bank will be uniform. Preferential rates could be offered only for deposits with higher amounts.

Number of withdrawals – limited (charges are levied if limits are exceeded). Such limits also vary from bank to bank.

For the purpose of financial inclusion, banks are also opening 'Basic Savings Bank Deposit Account (BSBDA) earlier known as 'no frill' accounts for people belonging to weaker section of the society. In some banks, the eligibility norm is limited to gross income of ₹ 5000 p.m. or less.

"Simplified Know Your Customer norms" are to be complied with for opening 'BSBDA – SMALL' account. Otherwise, BSBDA account would be subject to provisions of 'Prevention of Money Laundering Act/Rules and RBI instructions on KYC/AML for opening of bank accounts. BSBDA – SMALL account would be subject to the following conditions:

1. Total credits in such accounts not to exceed ₹ 1,00,000 in a year.
2. Maximum Balance in the account should not exceed ₹ 50,000 at any time.
3. Total of debits in the account not to exceed ₹ 10,000 in a month.
4. Such accounts are initially valid for 12 months which can be extended by another 12 months if the account holder submits proof of application for officially valid document.
5. No foreign remittance can be credited without completion of KYC formalities.

Example 1: Opening an SB Account

A person approaches you in the Bank to open a Savings Bank Account. How will you proceed?

Action Plan:

Talk to the person with warmth and cordiality for a few minutes and evaluate him/her through common sense. Ask him/her the purpose of opening the account. On satisfactory response, check the identity and address proof provided by him/her and take a self-attested Xerox of the documents. Obtain a passport size photograph of the account holder. Give him/her the account opening form for filling up and signature. SIGNATURE MUST BE DONE PREFERABLY IN FRONT OF YOU OR ANY OTHER BANK OFFICIAL.

However, in case of non-face-to-face customers, additional documents for risk mitigation may be insisted upon and first payment in such cases may be effected through customer's KYC compliant account with another Bank, if any. Having completed this, have the money deposited and open the account.

1.4 Current Account

This category of accounts is meant for business entities and organizations that need to have access to unrestricted number of withdrawals. The current account holders are not entitled to any interest on the deposits. This is a type of demand deposit from which withdrawals are permitted any number of times subject to availability of balance. No interest is allowed in current deposits.

Usually, minimum quarterly average balance (AQB) is ₹ 5000 and service charges are leviable for violation of minimum balance norm. Current and savings deposits together known as 'CASA' Deposits are much sought after business by all the banks as they are no cost or low cost deposits and contribute to bring down cost of funds for banks. Ideally, 45-50% of total deposits should be aimed at 'CASA' deposits. This is an area where public sector banks with number of branches in rural and semi-urban centres have an edge over private sector counterparts as rural and semi-urban centres offer a good scope for 'CASA' deposits.

With advent of technology, there are now number of variants of savings and current accounts where depending on Average Quarterly Balance, special value added services like, sweep-in, sweep-out facilities are rendered.

Some such products are:

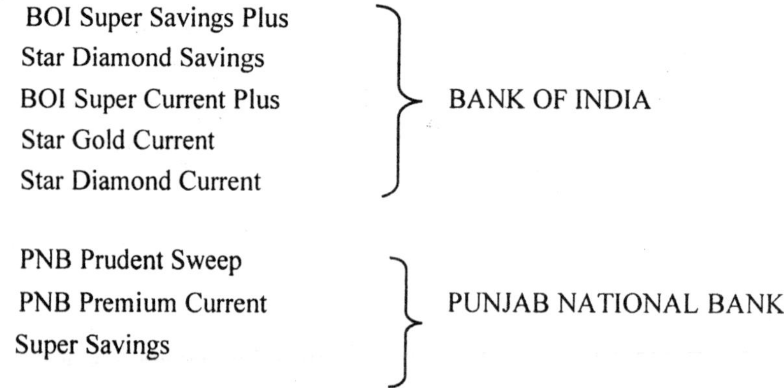

BOI Super Savings Plus
Star Diamond Savings
BOI Super Current Plus
Star Gold Current
Star Diamond Current
} BANK OF INDIA

PNB Prudent Sweep
PNB Premium Current
Super Savings
} PUNJAB NATIONAL BANK

Who Can Open?

Any person who is eligible to enter into contract and complies with KYC requirements.

This type of account can be opened in the name of two or more persons under the following mode of operations:

(a) Either or Survivor

(b) Jointly or Survivor

(c) Either or more of them or the Survivors

(d) 'Former' or 'Latter' or Survivor

Current account can also be opened by partnership firms, private and public limited companies, joint Hindu families, trusts, clubs etc. after submitting required documentations.

1.5 Requirements for Opening Account

(a) Forms to be signed by each applicant.

(b) Passport size photos of every account holder are required to be given to bank.

(c) KYC norms of RBI to be followed.

(d) In case of current account, KYC is not enough. It is advisable to follow KYC-B, i.e., Know Your Customers' Business. In short, you should politely enquire about type of business, duration, turnover, and other relevant aspects which will give all ideas about transaction.

(e) In case of partnership account, each partner's signature is to be obtained.

(f) In case of limited companies, Board Resolution along with Memorandum and Articles of Association to be obtained.

Deposits/Withdrawals

No restrictions in number of payments/withdrawals.

Closing of an Account

(a) Intention in writing must be given by the account holder to the Bank to close the account. Request letter in case of partnership firm should be submitted to bank duly signed by all the partners to close the account. In case of limited companies, a board resolution is required to submit to the Bank.

(b) Debit Cards, ATM cards, if any, along with unused Cheque leaves should be returned to bank while closing the account.

1.6 Term Deposits

Who Can Open?

Any person, proprietary concern, partnership firm, limited companies, clubs, Association, Trusts, Joint Hindu families, Government/Quasi Government bodies, Panchayats, Religious institutions, charitable institutes, municipalities approved by Bank can open Fixed Deposit Account. In this type of account, an amount remains fixed for a specified period. Companies, Clubs, Societies, Associations, and Educational Institutions etc. can also open such accounts.

Term deposits which are also known as Fixed Deposits or Time Deposits are usually allowed for a maximum duration of 120 months or 10 years.

Minimum duration is 7 days. Interest on Term Deposit is not regulated by Reserve Bank of India and is left free for Banks to decide.

Interests on Fixed deposits are paid at quarterly interval. Interest may also be paid to the customer at less than quarterly interval, e.g., monthly interval, but in that case the interest payment will be at monthly discounted rates. If interest is paid every quarter, the payment will be at actual rate contracted for the deposit – lower than that will qualify discounted rate and higher than quarterly will entitle at compounded rate – compounded quarterly.

Broad Features of Term Deposits

Premature withdrawal – by nature, a term deposit is a contract between a bank and depositor for investment of the amount at an agreed rate for a specific period. Hence, withdrawal before maturity does not come under right of the depositor but banks do allow breaking the deposit in case of customers' need. However, in such cases, interest as applicable at the time of opening and for the period the deposit has remained with the Bank will be allowed.

Renewal of Account

FD can be renewed on maturity. Renewal can be carried out at the prevailing interest rate on the maturity date, automatically if such auto-renewal instructions are given by the customer.

On the maturity, if the customer neither obtains payment nor renews the account, it is called as Overdue Fixed Deposit. If overdue period exceeds 14 days, interest would be paid to depositor and if the account is not renewed for a time equal to or more than overdue period, the interest rate applicable to Savings Bank deposit is payable on the deposit.

Example 2:

Mrs. Krishna opens a Fixed Deposit with ABC Bank on 1.1.2011 for 37 months for ₹ 1 lakh when interest rate structure was as follows:

Period	Interest Rates (per annum)
7 days to 14 days	3.75%
15 days to 45 days	4.75%
46 days to 179 days	5.25%
180 days to less than 1 year	6.25%
1 year to 3 years	8%
More than 3 years	9%

Mrs. Krishna faces a sudden requirement of funds and approaches the bank on 1.1.2012 for premature withdrawal of the deposit. In October 2011, interest rate underwent change only for the following periods:

1 year to 3 years	8.5%
More than 3 years	9.25%

In such scenario as an Officer in term deposit department, how would you deal with Mrs. Krishna's Fixed Deposit Account?

Ans: The deposit remained with the bank for 1 year. The deposit rate applicable for 1 year on 1.1.2012 is 8.5% p.a. but Mrs. Krishna opened the deposit account on 1.1.2011 when applicable rate for 1 year was 8% p.a. Hence, Mrs. Krishna will be entitled to 8% p.a., if no penalty is levied.

Future of Indian Banking is Very Bright for Retail Products

Indian consumer behaviour is changing. Urban household income has considerably gone up and will continue to grow in tune with India's GDP growth. India has a demographic advantage over other countries. More than 50% of populations are under 25 and about 70% below 35. This segment is likely to give a big push to consumption expenditure and retail loans – be it mortgage, auto or consumer loans. Technology also will support the increase in retail banking through introduction of convenience banking and internet banking, online transfer, mobile banking, store value cards and various other products. The increase in income will have a direct bearing on consumption patterns.

- **Automatic Renewal:** If instructions are given by the depositors at the time of opening the account, deposits get renewed automatically on maturity, for the same period, as that of the matured deposit but at the interest rate prevailing at the time of maturity.
- **Loan/Overdraft facility:** In case of urgent need of funds for a short period, the depositor can also avail the facility of Loan/Overdraft against the deposit. However, the loan amount/overdraft limit will vary from 75% to 90% of the deposit amount depending on the discretion of the bank.
- **Tax Implications:** Tax is deducted in Term Deposits at source on interest amount @ 10%., if interest income exceeds ₹ 10,000 for a customer in a financial year. However, in cases where PAN number is not provided, the rate of tax will be higher @ 20%. If the depositor is not a taxpayer and does not desire tax to be deducted from the interest amount, a declaration has to be filled in Form No. 15G/15H personally quoting PAN number in such declaration.

- Senior citizens are entitled to an additional interest rate of 0.50% irrespective of the amount of deposit.
- As in Savings and Current Deposit mentioned above, fixed deposits also are available with different banks with different value-added factors. Some such products are:

Double Benefit Deposits	BANK OF INDIA
Super Saver facility Sweep-in facility	} MANY BANKS

Recurring Deposits

Recurring deposit enables a depositor to save by paying into the account an agreed fixed sum monthly over a stipulated period. The deposits earn compound interest on quarterly basis. KYC norms for opening of account are applicable. The monthly installment should be minimum ₹ 500 in Metro and Urban branches and ₹ 100 or above in Semi-urban/Rural branches.

This account may be opened in the name of individuals, sole proprietorship concern, partnership firm, association, clubs, societies, trust, companies, etc. The illiterate, minor, blind persons are eligible to open account under this scheme.

Broad Features

- Recurring Deposit account can be opened for a minimum period of 12 months and thereafter upto a maximum period of 120 months.
- The amount of installment once fixed, cannot be changed.
- Installment is to be paid on or before the last working day of the month.

Advantages

1. Though a type of term deposit, interest on recurring deposit is not subject to TDS.
2. Monthly installment can be decided according to capacity and convenience of the depositor and based on a standing instructions, can be debited regularly from the savings account.

1.7 Certificates of Deposit

Certificates of Deposit (CDs) – Introduced in India in 1989

Features

It is a negotiable money market instrument.

Minimum amount of a CD should be ₹ 1 lakh, i.e., the minimum deposit that could be accepted from a single subscriber should not be less than ₹ 1 lakh and in the multiples of ₹ 1 lakh thereafter.

Investors in CDs could be individuals, corporations, companies, trusts, funds, associations etc. Non-resident Indians can also invest in CDs but on non-repatriable basis.

1. **Duration:** CDs can be issued for a minimum of 7 days and maximum of 1 year from the date of issue.

2. **Discount Rate**: CDs are issued at a discount on face value. The issuing bank is free to determine the discount rate.

3. **Floating rate:** CDs can also be issued at interest rate with a spread over an established benchmark, to be reset periodically.

   CDs being negotiable instrument are freely transferable by endorsement and delivery.

Format of negotiable CD is given below (Ref. RBI Master Circular – Guidelines for Issue of CDs – July 1, 2011):

Annex I

Format of Negotiable Certificate of Deposit (CD)

Name of the Bank/Institution

No.

₹ ________

Date ________

NEGOTIABLE CERTIFICATE OF DEPOSIT

________ Months/days after the date hereof, ________ <Name of the Bank/Institution> ________, at ________ <name of the place> ________, hereby promise to pay to ________ <name of the depositor> ________ or order the sum of Rupees ________ <in words> ______ only, upon presentation and surrender of this instrument at the said place, for deposit received.

For ________ <Name of the institution>________

Date of maturity ________ without days of grace.

Instructions	Endorsements	Date
	1.	
	2.	
	3.	
	4.	
	5.	

1.8 Non-Resident Deposit

1. **Ordinary Non-resident Accounts:** An account other than a Blocked or Non-resident (External) account maintained in Rupees with an authorized dealer by a non-resident person, firm, company or any other organization is called an Ordinary Non-resident Accounts. Any person who is residing outside India as well as Foreign Tourists on short visit to India may open NRO account.
2. **Permissible Debits and Repatriation:**
   - All local payments in rupees including payment for investments as specified by RBI and remittance outside India of current income like rent, dividend, pension etc.
   - Settlement of credit card holders.
3. **Resident Foreign Currency (RFC) Account:**
   - Returning NRIs may open a Resident Foreign Currency (RFC) Account with an authorized dealer in India and transfer balances held in NRE/FCNR(B) accounts.
   - Proceeds of assets held outside India at the time of return can be credited to RFC account.
   - The funds in RFC accounts are free from all restrictions regarding utilisation of foreign currency balances including any restriction on investment in any form outside India.
   - RFC accounts can be maintained in the form of current or savings or term deposit accounts.
4. **Resident Foreign Currency (Domestic) Account:**
   - An honorarium gift from a non-resident to settle any lawful obligation.
   - An honorarium gift during visit outside India.
   - Unspent amount of foreign exchange acquired from authorized persons for travel abroad.
   - Gifts received from close relatives, in foreign exchange.
5. **Non-resident (External) Accounts:** An account in Rupees opened and maintained with an authorized dealer specially permitted by the RBI under the Act, in the name of a person resident outside India in pursuance of the Non-resident (External) Accounts Rules 1970, is designated as a Non-resident (External) Account.

- NRE account may be in the form of savings, current, recurring or fixed deposit accounts. Such accounts can be opened only by the non-resident himself and not through the holder of the power of attorney.
- NRE accounts can be held jointly with other NRIs.
- Account will be maintained in Indian Rupees.
- Balances held in the NRE account are freely repatriable.
- Accrued interest income and balances held in NRE accounts are exempt from Income tax and Wealth tax, respectively.
- Authorized dealers/authorized banks may allow for a period of not more than two weeks, overdrawing in NRE savings bank accounts, up to a limit of ₹ 50,000 subject to the condition that such overdrawing together with the interest payable thereon are cleared/repaid within a period of two weeks, out of inward remittances through normal banking channels or by transfer of funds from other NRE/FCNR accounts.
- Savings – The interest rates on NRE Savings deposits shall be at the rate applicable to domestic savings deposits.
- Rate of Interest – Banks are free to determine interest rates of savings and term deposits of maturity of one year and above but cannot be generally higher than those offered on comparable domestic rupee deposits.
- Permissible credits to NRE account are inward remittance to India in permitted currency, proceeds of account payee cheques, demand drafts/bankers' cheques, issued against encashment of foreign currency, where the instruments issued to the NRE account holder are supported by encashment certificate issued by AD Category-I/Category-II, transfers from other NRE/FCNR accounts, interest accruing on the funds held in such accounts, interest on Government securities/dividends on units of mutual funds purchased by debit to the NRE/FCNR(B) account of the holder, certain types of refunds, etc.
- Eligible debits are local disbursements, transfer to other NRE/FCNR accounts of person eligible to open such accounts, remittance outside India, investments in shares/ securities/commercial paper of an Indian company, etc.
- Loans without any ceiling subject to usual margin requirements.
- Such accounts can be operated through power of attorney in favour of residents for limited purpose of withdrawal of local payments or remittances through normal banking channels to the account holder himself.

6. **Exchange Earners' Foreign Currency (EEFC) Accounts:**

- Exchange Earners' Foreign Currency (EEFC) is an account maintained in foreign currency with an Authorized Dealer. It is a facility provided to the foreign exchange earners, including exporters, to credit 100% of their foreign exchange earnings to the account, so that the account holders do not have to convert foreign exchange into Rupees and *vice versa*, thereby minimizing the transaction costs.
- All categories of foreign exchange earners, who are resident in India, may open EEFC accounts.
- An EEFC account can be held only in the form of a current account. No interest is payable on EEFC accounts.
- There is no restriction on withdrawal in Rupees of funds held in an EEFC account. However, the amount withdrawn in Rupees shall not be eligible for conversion into foreign currency and for re-credit to the account.

7. **Foreign Currency (Non-resident) Accounts (Banks):**

- FCNR(B) accounts are only in the form of term deposits for the period of 1 to 5 years.
- All debits/credits permissible in respect of NRE accounts are permissible in FCNR(B) accounts also.
- Account can be in Pound Sterling, US Dollar, Japanese Yen, Euro, Canadian Dollar, Australian Dollar, CHF, DKK, NZD, SEK.
- Minimum Deposit of USD 1,000 or equivalent.
- In case the depositor with any convertible currency other than designated currency desires to place a deposit in these accounts, authorized dealers may undertake with the depositor a fully covered swap in that currency against the desired designated currency. Such a swap may also be done between two designated currencies.
- Loans permissible subject to rules.
- The interest rates are stipulated by Reserve Bank of India. At present, in respect of FCNR(B) deposits of 1 to 3 years, interest shall be paid within the ceiling rate of LIBOR/SWAP rates plus 200 basis points and for deposits of 3-5 years interests will be applicable at LIBOR/SWAP rates plus 400 basis points.
- When an account holder becomes a person resident in India, deposits may be allowed to continue till maturity at the contracted rate of interest.

8. **Form QA 22:** While opening accounts in Indian rupees in the names of Indian branch/offices of foreign companies and foreign nationals residing in India, authorised dealers should obtain an undertaking in Form QA 22 signed by all personas authorised to operate the account.

   Form QA 22 is an undertaking given by the applicant that he will not make available to anyone in India, any foreign currency against reimbursement in Rupees.

   Form QA 22 is not required in the case of:

   (a) Foreign nationals of non-Indian origin permanently resident in India.

   (b) Foreign nationals of Indian origin.

   (c) Foreign embassies, consulates, other foreign Government establishments in India.

1.9 FOREIGN REMITTANCES

1. **Remittances Inward:** There is no restriction on receiving remittances in India from any foreign country. Foreign remittances may be in the form of mail transfers, TTs, DDs, Traveller's cheques etc. Any person in India can freely receive remittances from foreign country through an authorized dealer.

2. **Certificate for Inward Remittance:** An authorized dealer may issue a certificate either in foreign currency or in Rupee.

3. **Remittances Outward:** Remittances from India may be made by an authorized dealer against an application made in duplicate by a person on the Form A1 where the remittance is in connection with import of goods into India and/or on Form A2, for general remittances.

4. **Recurring Remittances:**

   - Wherever regular periodic remittances have to be made for purposes which are not covered by authorized dealers' authority, Reserve Bank issues in approved cases permits for recurring remittances on account of family maintenance, savings, maintenance of offices abroad, etc.

   - Foreign nationals who are not permanently resident in India but are in regular employment with Indian companies on monthly salary, are permitted to make recurring remittances for family maintenance.

   - Salaries to the employees deputed by foreign companies to their Indian offices may be paid abroad to the extent of 75% of the net salary and balance amount of salary may be paid in India.

Remittances Requiring Prior Permission of the Reserve Bank

1. Remittance of Break-bulk Agents Remunerations on Consolidation of Outward Sea/Air Cargo:

   (a) Freight forwarders undertaking consolidation of outbound cargo need services of break-bulk agents abroad. Sea cargo forwarders and IATA recognized Air cargo agents may approach a designated branch of an authorized dealer for remitting remuneration to break-bulk agents giving full particulars of the arrangements in Form BBX 1 together with a copy of the relative agency agreement. Authorized dealers may allow the remittance of remunerations to break-bulk agents on outward cargo on the basis of a Chartered Accountant's certificate to the effect that the amount of remittance applied for has been verified with reference to break-bulk agents debit notes/invoices, copy of Master Air-Way Bill (MAWB)/Master Bill of Lading (MBL) and original relative House Air-Way Bill (HAWB)/House Bill of Lading (HBL), as the case may be. Before allowing the remittance, authorized dealers may also obtain undertaking/certificate regarding payment of Income-tax and a statement in Form BBX2.

   (b) Air/Sea cargo agents are also permitted to pay freight to airlines/shipping companies in rupees in respect of exports made on FOB basis and recover the freight amount from the overseas consignee through their break-bulk agent abroad provided they undertake to repatriate the same to India through normal banking channels within a period of 30 days in case of Air Cargo and 90 days in case of Sea Cargo from the date of shipment.

   (c) Authorized dealer may call for Chartered Accountant's Certificate in form CAS to determine outstanding receivables. In cases where the receivables from an overseas agent outstanding for more than 6 months exceed U.S $ 2500, no remittance should be allowed without prior approval of Reserve Bank.

   (d) Authorized dealers should maintain systematic record of the remittances allowed together with documents called for which should be made available to their internal auditors/Reserve Bank officials as and when called for.

2. Cost of Euro Rail, etc. Passes/Tickets, Overseas Hotel Reservation
3. Operating Expenses of Indian Shipping Companies
4. Surplus Collections of Foreign Offline Carriers

5. Remuneration of Agents appointed Abroad by Indian Shipping Companies
6. Charter Hite of Foreign Ships/Aircrafts
7. Purchase of a Ship/Aircraft by Indian Airline/Shipping Company
8. Legacies/Bequests/Inheritances
9. Opening of Overseas Branch/Maintenance of an Overseas Branch
10. Advertisements Abroad

Free Remittances

1. **Commission to Buying Agents Abroad:**
   (a) Of Importers: The amount of commission may be remitted to the buying agent abroad against an application from the importer.
   (b) Of Exporters: The amount of commission may be remitted against an application by letter from the exporter.
2. **Value of Import under Penalty:** The value of an import under penalty may be remitted to the overseas exporter by an authorized dealer.
3. **War Risk Insurance Premium/Bunker or Congestion Surcharge/Premium for Extended Insurance Cover:** The amounts in these cases may be remitted to the respective payees.
4. **Surplus Passage and Freight Collections of Foreign Airline Companies:** The surplus passage and freight collections of foreign airline companies may be remitted to its non-resident owners by the authorized dealers with which the company maintains its bank account in India.
5. **Surplus Passage and Freight Collections of Foreign Shipping Companies:** The surplus passage and freight collections of foreign shipping companies may be remitted to its non-resident owners to the extent of its ad hoc remittance entitlement by the authorized dealer with which the company maintains its bank accounts.
6. **Passage Fare in Rupees of Foreign Airline/Shipping Companies:** A foreign airline/shipping company can freely accept passage fare in rupees:
   (a) From residents for their own travel from and to India
   (b) From non-residents for their travel out of India
   (c) From the crew members of a foreign shipping company
7. **Expenses towards Dry-docking/Repair of Ship/Survey Fees/Purchase of Spares incurred Abroad:** Remittances to meet the expenses incurred abroad on account of any one or more of the above may be made by an authorized dealer against an application on Form A2.

8. Remittances for Other Purposes:

(a) Consular Fees

(b) Casual Remittances

(c) Royalty on Books

(d) Royalty on Software Imports

(e) Cost of Services rendered by Overseas Parties

(f) Donations by residents

(g) Electronic Data-based costs

(h) Repairing Charges of Defective Goods

(i) Export Claims

(j) Controlling Charges, Legal Expenses etc.

(k) Participation in Trade/Book Fairs and Exhibitions Abroad

(l) Bids in Foreign Currency for Projects to be executed in India

Gold Card Scheme for Exporters

Gold Card Scheme for exporters was introduced in the Exim Policy 2003-04 allowing creditworthy exporters with good track record easy access to export credit on best terms. The scheme is under review by a technical committee of Reserve Bank of India headed by Mr. G. Padmanabhan, ED, RBI.

Features of Gold Card Scheme

(i) All creditworthy exporters, including those in small and medium sectors with good track record would be eligible for issue of Gold Card by individual banks as per the criteria to be laid down by the latter.

(ii) Banks would clearly specify the benefits they would be offering to Gold Card holders.

(iii) Requests from card holders would be processed quickly by banks within 25 days/15 days and 7 days for fresh applications/renewal of limits and adhoc limits, respectively.

(iv) 'In-principle' limits would be set for a period of 3 years with a provision for stand-by limit of 20 per cent to meet urgent credit needs.

(v) Card holders would be given preference in the matter of granting of packing credit in foreign currency.

(vi) Banks would consider waiver of collaterals and exemption from ECGC guarantee schemes on the basis of card holder's creditworthiness and track record.

(vii) The concessive rate of interest on post-shipment rupee export credit applicable upto 90 days may be extended for a maximum period upto 365 days.

1.10 Retail Loans

Retail lending is the practice of lending to individuals and small and medium borrowers. Retail loans have taken a prominent role in the lending activities of banks, as the availability of credit and the number of products offered for retail lending has grown. The amounts advanced through retail loans are usually smaller than those lent to corporates. Retail loans are mainly provided for purposes of buying a house (home loans), car (auto loans), personal needs like buying a white good (consumer loans), personal loans and educational loans.

1. **Retail Loans – Characteristics:**
   - These are small ticket loans (There is no hard and fast definition for small).
   - These loans meet the needs of a large number of customers with well diversified portfolios.
   - The customers are generally individuals or small organizations.
   - These loans offer standard ready-to-use products to customers. Customers' requirements are usually not customized.
   - Credit decisions for such loans are quick and more streamlined.
   - Large number of transactions and high volume.
   - Transactions being high, supervision and monitoring costs are also high.
   - Interest yield is relatively higher.
2. **Evaluating Credit Process:** Credit analysis leads to identification of lender's risk in making a loan. There is a five-stage process for evaluation:
   (a) Identification of the applicant
   (b) Overview of management experience, operations and firm/industry.
   (c) Financial analysis – ratios, cash flow and funds flow as may be deemed necessary.
   (d) Final interview with the proponent focusing mainly on need based finance, actual use of finance and source of repayment.
   (e) Repayment Capacity.
3. **Business and Industry Outlook:** Along with evaluation, the credit officer also examines historical sales growth and the relationship between

industry sales and the business cycle. In case of a new unit, careful study of the industry and its future as also the feasibility of the projected growth of the proposed unit is very important.

Types of Standard Retail Loans:

1. Housing Loans
2. Personal Loans
3. Vehicle Loans
4. Education Loans
5. Loans to SMEs

1.11 Housing Loan

It is an arrangement in which a lender gives money to a borrower for construction of a house/purchase of a flat/plot of land/renovation/extension of the existing house and the borrower agrees to repay the money, along with interest, during an agreed period.

Broadly, loans are given for the following purpose:

(a) Construction or outright purchase of a residential house

(b) Purchase of new/old/unfinished house/flat

(c) Purchase of plot of land and constructing house thereon

(d) Repairs/renovation/modification, extension of the existing house

(e) Furnishing of the house-purchase of consumer durables.

1. **Eligibility:** Banks determine eligibility based on repayment capacity, income and age. Other factors such as qualification, length of service/occupation also play an important role. The eligibility for acquiring a home loan is augmented by clubbing income of father/spouse/mother/son, by clearing outstanding debts, by stretching loan tenure etc. Salaried individuals can increase their eligibility by showing their performance linked income or bonus earned.

   Most of the banks and FIs have laid down minimum eligibility norms which normally are:

(a) An Indian resident or NRI

(b) Age:

- Minimum: 21 years
- Maximum: Age of retirement for salaried class and 70 years for others.

(c) Salaried, self-employed or businessmen having regular income with documentary source of income

2. Quantum of Loan – Varies from Bank to Bank But Usually

- For construction of a house/flat at metro centers – maximum ₹ 500 lakh.
- At other centres – maximum ₹ 300 lakh.
- For repair/renovation/extension/addition to house/flat – maximum ₹ 50 lakh.
- For furnishing the house/flat – maximum ₹ 5 lakh.

Amount of loan eligibility depend on gross monthly salary/gross annual income based on I/T returns, salary certificate etc.

Some banks have special housing finance schemes for high net worth individuals where loan amount can exceed ₹ 5 crore maximum upto ₹ 25 crore (subject to xxxxx times, e.g., 5 times of the gross income shown in the latest income tax return/order).

In case of individuals, a relationship is maintained between net take home pay/income (net of equated monthly installment on the proposed loan) and gross pay/income – usually a minimum of 40%.

Loan to value ratio/margin (varies from Bank to Bank and borrower to borrower): Usually for the first house, 80% of the cost of the project, i.e., 20% margin.

3. **Nature of Loan:** Term Loan.

4. **Interest Rates:** Interest rates may be levied on fixed rate or floating rate basis.

(a) **Fixed Rate Loan:** As the name suggests, fixed interest rate loans enable borrowers to stick to repayments in fixed equal installments over the entire period of the loan. Interest rate in such cases is fixed and does not vary with market fluctuations. Fixed rate home loans bring an element of certainty. The downside is that fixed rate loans are usually higher than floating rates by a margin of 1% to 2% and in the event of reduction in market interest rates, the borrower does not get the benefit. But one needs to ascertain at the time of taking loan if the fixed rate is really fixed or fixed for only certain number of years.

(b) **Floating Rate Loan:** Floating rate loans are tied up to a base rate plus a margin which is why the rate keeps floating as and when base rate undergoes change. Floating rates are generally cheaper than fixed rates by about 1%-2% giving borrowers a cushion to absorb some rise in rates. For example, borrower X has availed a loan at 14% fixed rate whereas borrower Y has availed floating rate at 1.5% over base rate when base rate is 10.5% p.a. In such case even if base rate goes up by 1% to 1.5%, the borrower is not worse off vis-à-vis fixed rate holder. The difficulty with floating rate is the uncertainty about the quantum of EMI as fixed income earners will have very hard time to make up for extra loan of EMI if interest rates goes up.

However, majority of borrowers go for floating rate loans as both for borrowers and lenders fixed rates pose a risk especially for long-tenure loans.

5. **Annual reducing basis:** Under this practice, the borrower goes on repaying equated monthly installment (EMI) but a portion of the principal which has been repaid would also attract interest till the end of the year because the principal reduces only at the year end.
6. **Monthly reducing basis:** Under this system, the principal gets reduced at the interval of every month upon payment of EMI. EMI in monthly reducing system is lesser than that of annual reducing system.
7. **Daily reducing basis:** Under this system, the principal gets reduced from the day the EMI is paid. EMI in daily reducing system is lesser than that of monthly reducing system.
8. **EMI:** This represents monthly installment amount the borrower should pay till full repayment. The amount of EMI consists of both principal and interest component and repayment towards principal increases with the passage of time. This is why, during initial years, borrower does not find much reduction in principal as large portion of the EMI goes towards interest repayment.
9. **EMI calculations:** EMI calculations take into account the following:

   1. Amount of Loan
   2. Interest Rate
   3. Tenure of the Loan

   Thus, the formula would be: (P × i) (1 + i) ^ N/{ (1 + i) ^ N } – 1

   where,

   P = Amount of Loan

   I = Interest rate divided by 12

   ^ = Raised to (to the power of)

   N = Tenure in months

Example 3:

As per EMI calculation formula: (P × i) (1 + i) ^ N/{ (1 + i) ^ N } – 1, what would be the EMI if

Loan Amount : ₹ 40 lakh

Interest Rate : 10% p.a. (payable in 15 years)

Ans: EMI = (40,00,000 × .10/12) × { (1 + .10/12) ^ 180 }/{ (1 + .10/12) ^ 180} – 1

= (40,00,000 × .00833) × {(1.00833)^ 180}/{(1 + .00833) ^ 180} – 1

= 33,320 × 4.45127 / (4.45127 – 1)

= 148316.32 / 3.45127

= 42974.42

EMI is ₹ 42,974.

10. **Teaser Rates:** Under this scheme, banks provide credit at lower rates for first few years and subsequently raise the interest rates. Teaser rates 'tease' customers into applying for a home loan. Offers are made by lenders at low introductory rates which tempts customers to avail of more and more home loans. But the low rates which are fixed for initial few number of years will change into a floating market related rate which could be significantly higher. Such practices are prone to attracting sub-prime borrowers. Quite a few banks in India led by State Bank of India introduced teaser rates but Reserve Bank of India got apprehensive about the fallout of this practice in increasing lending to less creditworthy borrowers resulting in future defaults and foreclosures. Both the lenders and borrowers should be confident of increasing repayment capacity of the borrower with the passage of time.

11. **Processing Fee:** Amount required to be paid to lender being the cost of processing of the request varies from bank to bank usually around 0.25% to 0.50% of the loan amount but subject to a ceiling.

(i) Pre-payment Penalty: Pre-payment of the loan, i.e., payment before the due date is permitted. In case of floating rate loans, banks do not usually charge any pre-payment penalty but in case of fixed interest loans, penalty is levied.

(ii) Security:

(a) Principal security is the Equitable/Registered Mortgaged of the property purchased out of bank funds taken. The title of the property should be clear and marketable for which a certificate has to be obtained from banks' approved lawyer. In case, a salaried borrower has already availed loan from his/her organization, a second or *Pari Passu* charge over the property will be required.

(b) In addition, banks may insist on some collateral security like Fixed Deposit, Insurance Policy, Share Certificates or other liquid certificates.

12. Other Features:

Repayment Period: Usually maximum of 25 years or the age of retirement in case of salaried persons and 65/70 years for others including moratorium period, if any, which usually is 18/24 months. Interest rate is linked with the amount of loan and also tenure of repayment.

Example 4: Floating Rate

Repayment Period	**Amount**		
	Upto ₹ 25 lakh	**Above ₹ 25 lakh but below ₹ 75 lakh**	**₹ 75 lakh and above**
Upto 5 years	0.5% above Base Rate	1.25% above Base Rate	1.5% above Base Rate
Over 5 years upto 15 years	0.75% above Base Rate	1.5% above Base Rate	1.75% above Base Rate
Over 15 years upto 25 years	1% above Base Rate	1.75% above Base Rate	2% above Base Rate

Field Investigation

Even after due diligence and verification of records like salary/income, valuation by an approved valuer, search of the title deed with the office of sub-registrar by an approved lawyer, field investigation by a bank's officer is a must. There had been in the past number of frauds leading to fictitious housing loans causing huge loss of banks' funds and avoidable loss of time and energy of staff in unearthing the fraud. Field investigation should include personal verification of the residential unit/plot to be purchased (including market enquiry from neighboring shops, business units or any other permanent dwellers about the credentials of the unit), visit to the existing place of residence of the applicant as also the workplace of the applicant. In case of joint applications, if both the applicants are employed, visit to each of the applicant's workplace is necessary.

Credit Investigation Report

Bank is authorized to make enquiries from any of the Credit Information Bureau like CIBIL and obtain credit information. Bank is also authorized to disclose information pertaining to the loan to Credit Bureau approved by RBI or Govt. of India.

Reserve Bank of India has accorded approval to four companies for setting-up credit information agency:

(a) Credit Information Bureau (India) Ltd.

(b) Equifax Credit Information Services Pvt. Ltd.

(c) Experian Credit Information Company of India Pvt. Ltd.

(d) Highmark Credit Information Services Pvt. Ltd.

Security Documents

Broadly, the following are the security documents generally being obtained by the bank after sanction but before disbursement:

(a) Demand Promissory Note

(b) Home Loan Agreement

(c) Equitable mortgage of the property (oral assent) – signature of the borrower(s) in the attendance register (in case the mortgage is equitable or else registered mortgage)

(d) Installment letter

(e) Singular or Joint and several guarantee document, if applicable

(f) Post dated cheques/standing instructions to debit account, as applicable

(g) Insurance of the building against risk of fire, earthquake, floods etc. Policy should be in the name of the respective bank account – the borrower/s

Identity/Residence Proof

- Passport
- Voter ID card
- PAN Card
- Ration Card
- Any other proof to the satisfaction of the bank

Investment Proof (If Applicable)

- Bank statement for the last six months of all operating and salary accounts
- Bank statements for the last six months of all current accounts, if self-employed
- Any other photocopies of investments held, if required by the bank

Property Title Proof/Other Documents

- Original Sale agreement with Builder/Developer duly registered, Registration receipt.
- Photocopies of title deeds, if applicable.
- A certificate from builder's Chartered Accountant certifying that the builder has not mortgaged the property anywhere else .
- Certified true copy of approved plan.
- Copies of receipts of payments made to the builder/developer.
- Allotment letter.
- Possession letter.
- Lease agreement, if applicable (property bought from a development authority).
- No Objection Certificate from the developer, society or development authority as applicable.
- In case of alternate or additional security, documents for the same depending upon the security details.
- Approved plans and clearance certificates along with estimates, if applicable.

1.12 Vehicle Loan

Vehicle loan is poised to grow at a high rate in view of great potential of 4-wheeler and 2-wheeler loans in the ensuing decade. Consumption boom among younger segment of population will give a boost to demand for such loans.

The number of banks and institutions offering vehicle loans in India is on the upswing. Car finance companies offer up to 90% of the cost of the car, if it is new and 85% of the cost of the car, if it is an used car. This again is decided based on the repayment period and the model of the car.

Two-wheeler Loan

1. **Eligibility:** All resident Indians within age bracket of 21-65 years – salaried, professionals, self-employed, businessmen, farmers, pensioners are eligible for a two-wheeler loan. Companies, partnership firms, other corporate entities except HUF are also eligible.

2. **Purpose:** Purchase of a new or second hand two-wheeler (second hand vehicle should not be usually more that 3 years old).

3. **Quantum of Loan:** Varies from case to case – but usually a maximum ceiling of ₹ 100,000/- which is related to income either based on salary or Income Tax Return (e.g., 24 times of monthly gross emoluments or twice gross average annual income). Monthly take home salary for salaried persons or monthly average in case of others taking into account all deductions/EMI for all loans including the loan under consideration should not usually be less than 40% of the monthly gross salary/monthly average income.

4. **Rate of Interest:** Varies from time to time and bank to bank.

5. **Margin:** Varies from case to case but ranges from 5% to 25%. In case of second hand vehicles, it may go upto 40%.

6. **Processing Charge:** 0.25% to 1.25% subject to a minimum and maximum or in such cases a lump sum amount.

7. **Security:**
   (i) Hypothecation of the vehicle purchased out of Bank finance.
   (ii) Charge to be registered with the R.T.O. with Bank clause.
   (iii) Third party guarantee or any other collateral (not mandatory).

8. **Repayment Period:** Usually a maximum of 60 months – generally ranges from 48-60 months.

Four-wheeler Loan

1. **Eligibility:** Similar to two-wheeler loan.

2. **Quantum:** Amount related to gross income – either from salary or from business. Usually in the range of twice/thrice gross annual income subject to a ceiling of ₹ 100 lakh.

3. **Repayment:**
   - For new vehicle – 84 months
   - For second hand vehicle – 36 months

4. **Margin:**
   - New vehicles – 15% to 20%
   - Second hand vehicles – 40% to 50%
5. **Age:**
   - Minimum: 21 years
   - Maximum: Repayment period not to exceed retirement age in case of salaried persons and 65 years in case of others.
6. **Rate of Interest:** Varies between 0.5% to 2% over base rate depending on the length of repayment period and amount of the loan.

   Example:
   - For loans upto 5 years – 2.5% over Base Rate
   - For loans over 5 years – 3% over Base Rate

   Quantum/Repayment/Margin/ROI would, however, vary from bank to bank.

1.13 Personal Loans

Banks have different schemes for personal loans suiting to needs of various stages of life. Of course, while some schemes are commonly favourable with most of the banks, some are unique to a particular bank.

(i) Loans for expenses towards coaching/tuition fee for preparation towards entrance examination of professional courses, e.g., in medicine, engineering, management, accountancy etc.

(ii) If the student is successful in securing admission, there are established well-circulated schemes for educational loan in almost all the banks.

(iii) Upon completion of the professional education, the student secures a job. If he/she is in need of funds for marriage expenses, banks, subject to repayment capacity and eligibility criteria can give loans for marriage expenses.

(iv) Holiday Loan Scheme to meet expenses like airfare/train fare/accommodation/sight-seeing excursions etc.

(v) Thereafter comes the need for home loans which is an well-established scheme.

(vi) Specially focused schemes like, loan scheme for the physically challenged for purchase of sophisticated aids, tools/appliances for promotion of their rehabilitation (Example: Star Mitra Personal Loan of Bank of India).

(vii) Loans to customers drawing regular pensions/family pensions through the same branch where loan is sought for various personal purposes like medical expenses, education or marriage expenses of children or any other personal expenses of bonafide nature.

1. **Eligibility:** Salaried employees, professionals and self-employed, pensioners, any other resident Indians with acceptable net worth.
2. **Loan Amount:** Usually ranges between ₹ 10,000 to ₹ 2,00,000 but depending on the repayment capacity, the purpose/need and the collateral security offered, Banks lend higher amount which may go upto ₹ 10 lakh. Eligibility of the amount is related to monthly emoluments in case of salaried employee or gross annual income as per IT Return for others.
3. **Purpose:** Marriage expenses of self, children or even dependant near relative, medical expenses, education expenses (separate scheme for educational loan is also existing), repair/renovation of existing house/flat (beyond what is permissible under housing loan scheme), purchase of consumer durables, any other bonafide personal expenses approved by the Bank.
4. **Repayment:** Ranges from 36 to 60 equated monthly installments.
5. **Security:** Personal loans are given both on secured as well as clean basis.

   Secured Loans are given against:

   - Hypothecation charge on acquired assets
   - Any other collateral as may be offered and accepted, e.g., National Savings Certificates, Shares, Assignment of LIC Policies, mortgage of House properties etc.

1.14 Educational Loan

Most of the banks in India provide educational loans. This scheme aims at provision of financial support on affordable terms and conditions to the deserving/meritorious students for pursuing higher studies in India and abroad.

Though educational loans are primarily aimed at financing higher education in India and abroad, some banks also offer schemes for school education covering studies from Nursery to XIIth standard. These loans are given to parents of students who:

1. Are resident Indians.
2. Have secured admission to a recognized schools.

For higher education, the coverage of courses are very wide. Eligible courses include:

1. Graduation courses
2. Post Graduation and Doctorate courses
3. Professional courses like Engineering, Medical, Agriculture, Management, C.A., ICWA
4. Courses approved by UGC/Govt./AICTE etc.
5. Approved courses offered in India by reputed foreign universities.

Courses Eligible for Study Abroad

1. Post Graduation: MCA/MBA/MS etc.
2. Any job-oriented technical professional courses offered by reputed universities.
3. Regular degree/diploma courses like Aeronautical, shipping, pilot training from approved institutions.

Any student who is a resident Indian and has secured admission to an approved course and has a good academic record is eligible for the loan. Father/mother should join as co-borrower.

Coverage of Expenses

Expenses that are covered under educational loans include:

(a) Tuition fees payable to the Institution including hostel

(b) Examination/Laboratory/Library fee

(c) Purchase of books/equipments/instruments

(d) Caution money deposit

(e) Passage money for studies abroad

(f) Purchase of computers

(g) Insurance cover for the student

(h) Any other expenses that may be necessary for completion of the course

Quantum of Finance

- **Usually for studies in India:** Maximum of ₹ 10 lakh

  studies Abroad: Maximum of ₹ 20 lakh
- **Margin:** Upto ₹ 4 lakh – NIL. Above ₹ 4 lakh – varies between 5% to 15%

- **Security:**

  (i) Upto ₹ 4 lakh – No security to be insisted upon

  (ii) > ₹ 4 lakh < ₹ 7.5 lakh – An acceptable third party guarantee and assignment of future income.

  (iii) > ₹ 7.5 lakh – Tangible security equal to the entire loan amount and assignments of future income.

Repayment Period

Usually, there is a moratorium period for the entire course tenure plus a reasonable time of 1 year or securing a job whichever is earlier. Thereafter, the loan is repayable in 5 -7 years.

Rate of Interest

Varies from time to time and bank to bank but usually there is a concession on interest charged during the moratorium period (e.g., simple interest/1% concession if interest paid during moratorium period etc.). Maximum rate generally goes upto 3% above Base Rate.

1.15 Reverse Mortgage Loan

Senior citizens, many a times, may have assets in the form of house property but no cash to survive. At the same time, if they dispose of the house, they do not have a place to stay. Reverse mortgage loan is an answer to this problem. As the name suggests, it is opposite to a typical mortgage like home loan. In a home loan, customer borrows money in the beginning and then make repayments by way of installments over the repayment tenure and the property purchased out of the loan stands mortgaged to the lender. But, in a reverse mortgage, an existing property free from any encumbrance is given to the lender by way of mortgage and lender would, in turn, give money by way of series of installments or in lump sum as mutually decided. During the entire period of loan, payments are received from the bank, and the borrower and/or his spouse resides in the house. The scheme was launched in 2009.

Basic Features of the Scheme

- A home owner above 60 years of age is eligible for reverse mortgage loan.
- The property should be free from any encumbrance with a clear title.
- Borrower is not required to make any repayment during his lifetime. Only statutory dues like taxes need to be paid.

- Reverse mortgage loans are extended by scheduled banks and Housing finance companies. The loan can be given to the borrower by way of monthly/quarterly/half-yearly/annual installments or lump sum or as a combination of all of these.
- Quantum of loan is based on several factors – namely the age of the borrower, market value of the property, market interest rates, pattern of disbursement preferred by the borrower etc. Usually, higher the age and higher the value of property, higher is the permissible amount of loan.
- Valuation of the property is done at periodic intervals and Bank would be free to revise the tenure or amount of the loan based on such revaluation.
- Married couples can avail of the facility as joint borrowers but one of them at least has to be above 60 years of age.
- The loan will be due for repayment in the event of:
  (a) The death of the last surviving borrower
  (b) Sale of the property
  (c) Moving out of the house permanently by the borrower.
- Upon death of the home owner, the legal heirs may choose to retain or sell the house. In the event of sale of the house, the entire outstanding against the loan account has to be repaid out of the sale proceeds and surplus, if any, will be received by the legal heirs.
- Maximum period of the loan: Lifetime of the borrower(s).
- The borrower or his heirs can repay/prepay with accrued interest at any point of time during the tenure of the loan.
- The government has also allowed insurance companies to lend under the scheme.

For example:

A senior citizen, owns a house which is valued at ₹ 1 crore. He or she can avail of a reverse mortgage loan of ₹ 80 lakh on the house being 80% of the value of the house. Entire amount is not disbursed in one lump sum. Owner can get 50% of the loan amount or ₹ 15 lakh whichever is lower as a lump sum. Rest will be disbursed as annuity. Amount of annuity varies from bank to bank and depends on the period for which owner wants the annuity. Usually for a reverse mortgage loan of 20 years, it comes to ₹ 100 per month for every ₹ 1 lakh reverse mortgage value. Annuity income from reverse mortgage loan will be tax-free.

1.16 CARDS

Cards are commonly used by customers as financial services. There are various types of cards. Some of the important categories of cards are as follows:

Charge Card

Charge card enables a customer to charge payments on account of purchases etc. to the card over a specific period (billing cycle) and pay the balance in full on the expiry of the period. Balance cannot be carried over to the next cycle. Charge cards do not usually have any pre-set credit limit and there is no spending limit but full payment needs to be made at the end of the period. Hence, there is no scope of interest charges. There is an annual fee which in some cases is waived during first year. Applicant need to have a very good credit score in order to be eligible for a charge card.

Credit Card

Credit cards allow holders to carry over the outstanding upon payment of a minimum amount. This is where the concept of credit comes in and the outstanding balance also carries interest which ranges between 1.5% to 3% p.m. Credit card comes with a pre-set spending limit which also includes a smaller percentage of cash withdrawal. The rate of interest on cash withdrawal may be higher than the carry over amount of purchases besides a fee. There are various choices of cards depending on income criteria, credit score and other eligibility criteria. Some issuers offer 0% interest on balance transfers upto a specified period but with a processing fee. Majority of the card issuers are either linked with Master Card or Visa.

Debit Card

A type of card which debits cardholder's account immediately the transaction is undertaken. In case the amount of transaction exceeds available clear balance, the transaction is rejected. Cardholder can purchase items from merchant establishments or in case of requirement of cash, can go to nearest ATM and can draw cash.

While issuing a debit card, Bank does not need to make credit checks as no credit is allowed and there is hardly any possibilities of bad debt. For a customer, it is convenience as there is no need to carry cash and if cash is required, nearest ATM would serve the purpose.

ATM Card

ATM Cards are also plastic cards with a magnetic strip/with a chip. Along with ATM card, customer is provided a PIN (Personal Identification Number). Insertion of card in the ATM and keying in the current PIN would complete the transaction. Generally, the following services are performed at an ATM:

1. Deposit/withdrawals of cash
2. Balance Enquiry
3. Funds Transfer (for the same customer at different centres)
4. Making Bill Payments like telephone, electricity etc.
5. Cheque Book Requisitions
6. Statement of account for limited transactions (mini statement)
7. Change of PIN.

Most ATMs are connected to interbank networks enabling people to withdraw money from any ATM. It is not necessary that the customer has to approach only the ATM of the Bank where account is maintained.

ATMs are known in various names in different countries, e.g., Bank Machine (Canada), Drink Link (Ireland), Cash Machine (New Zealand), Hole in the Wall (Australlia), Bancomat (Russia).

ATMs owned by private parties are known as 'White Lable ATMs'.

1.17 Internet Banking

Modern Banking has enabled customers to use technology for financial services. One of the most commonly used delivery channel amongst new generation urban/metro customers is Internet Banking. Internet Banking provides:

- 24 hour banking services
- Connectivity throughout the world
- Speed and accuracy
- Unlimited access and lesser hassels
- Effective marketing tool

The following services can be easily availed through internet banking:

(a) Balance inquiry/view account transactions.

(b) Fill up account opening request.

(c) Request for Cheque book.

(d) Bill payments/Tax payments/IRCTC.

(e) Stop payment requests.

(f) Funds transfer.

(g) E-mail statement of accounts.

(h) Request for debit cards.

(i) ASBA facility.

(j) Corporates can view trade-finance related facilities.

For Internet Banking facilities, all that one needs is a Personal computer and an internet connections. User connects to Bank's website through internet, logs in through valid user id, password and additional security code.

Internet Banking has transformed banking anywhere 24 × 7, much faster and with greater accuracy.

However, security related issues pose a threat as hackers and other fraudsters have been cheating the genuine customers by withdrawing money from the accounts. This is a risk management issue for the banks as well as regulator. Customers must be careful to ensure secrecy of user id, password and other account details.

1.18 Electronic Clearing Service

ECS is an electronic mode of receipts and payments relating to trasactions which are common and repetitive in nature. Bulk payment of amounts towards dividend, interest, salary, pension or bulk collection of telephone, electricity, water charges, collections of loan installments etc. are all effected through ECS. This amounts to transfer of funds from one account to many accounts or *vice versa*. Hence, this is broadly of two types – ECS credit and ECS debit. Transactions relating to debit to many accounts and credit to one (e.g., electricity, telephone bill, payment of insurance premium etc.) would come under ECS debit. Transactions relating to payment of dividend, interest, salary, pension necessitating debit to one account and credit to many will come under ECS credit.

Under ECS credit, the beneficiary needs to give a mandate to the institutions with his/her consent to avail the ECS facility with full details of the bank, branch account and authorises the institution to credit the account with the branch. In case of any change in the particulars of the account, the beneficiary must advise the institution of such changes.

Similarly, in respect of ECS debit, the customer needs to authorize the bank branch to recover the amount at the stated periodic interval. The mandate is also to be duly verified by the beneficiary's bank.

The user institution has to register with an ECS centre and needs to submit relevant details of the customers (name, bank, branch, account number, MICR code of the destination, bank branch etc., desired date of debit to customer's account in a format to the ECS centre).

ECS debit scheme offers many advantages to customers, user institutions as well as to the Banking system.

Advantages of ECS Debit Schemes to the Customers

1. Takes care of automatic debit to customer account on the due dates.
2. Customers need not to keep track record of due date for payments.
3. Debits are monitored by the ECS users, and the customers alerted accordingly.
4. Cost-effective.

Benefits of ECS Debit Schemes to User Institutions

1. Savings on administrative machinery and costs of collecting the cheques from customers, presenting in clearing.
2. Better cash management because of realization/recovery of dues on due dates.
3. Avoids chances of loss, theft of instruments in transit, etc.
4. Realisation of payments on a uniform date instead of fragmented receipts spread over many days.
5. Cost-effective.

Advantages of ECS Debit Schemes to the Banking System

1. No paper handling.
2. Easy processing. Process can be completed with minimal manual intervention.
3. Smooth process of reconciliation for the sponsor banks.
4. Cost-effective.

1.19 MOBILE BANKING

Mobile Banking is one more alternative delivery channel which allows banking anytime, anywhere through mobile phone. One can access banking information, enter into transactions in various accounts, transfer funds, pay bills and even recharge mobile phone or book movie tickets. This is a simple, secure, convenient anytime, anywhere banking.

Some of the categories of service provided by some banks are as follows:

Mobile Banking service over wireless application protocol (WAP) – This service is rendered through Java enabled/Android mobile phones (with or without GPRS)/i-phones – the user is required to download the software to the mobile handset. Customers, irrespective of their telecom service provider, can avail of this service provided they are current or saving account holders – however, there would be a limit for per day transaction at the initial stage.

In case of mobile banking over SMS, all phones irrespective of GPRS connections or Java/non-Java can be used upon payment of only SMS charges.

The following services can be availed:

(a) Balance enquiry

(b) Mobile top up

(c) Mobile to mobile transfer

(d) Change MPIN

Subject to a per-day transaction limit, per customer per day, all current/savings account holders can avail this service.

Banks, however, are permitted to offer mobile banking services upon getting necessary clearance from the Department of Payment and Settlement Systems, Reserve Bank of India.

All banks who have implemented core banking solutions are allowed to provide mobile banking services.

Customers having mobile phones of any network should be able to avail the service which means that this service should be network neutral.

Transaction Limit

Though under RBI Guidelines (Circular No. DPSS.CO.PD.No. 1098/02.23.001/2011-12 of 22/12/2011), there should not be any limit for transactions involving purchase of goods and services, banks may take a view in terms of respective risk perspection and put in place Board approved limit.

Remittance of Funds for Cash Disbursement

Banks are allowed to provide fund transfer services from the accounts of customers for delivery in cash to transferees. Disbursal of funds to recipient can be facilitated through any authorized agent appointed by the Bank (e.g., Business Correspondent) or even at ATMs. It is not mandatory for the recipient to be an account holder. However, such transfers will be subject to certain restrictions as follows:

(a) Maximum value of such cash transfers will be ₹ 10,000 per transaction. Banks may put some cap on a periodic basis.

(b) Disbursement of funds at the agent/ATM will be only after identification of the recipient. Authorized agents must undergo a process of due diligence before appointment.

Technology and security standards are of paramount importance. Banks must follow appropriate security standards as mobile banking services are mostly technology enabled. Some minimum standards are laid down in RBI Guidelines (Master Circular – Mobile Banking of 2013, Annexure I). Customer Protection Issues are also equally important.

Mobile banking, in particular, is fraught with higher risks for banks not meeting the secrecy/customer-confidentiality obligations. Very clear contracts should be drawn up between the payee and payees' bank, the participating bank and service provider defining rights and obligations of each party.

Chapter 2 CORPORATE LOANS

2.1 Fund-based Facilities

Loans extended by banks are either fund-based or non-fund based. Any facility involving outlay of funds is grouped under fund-based facility. As such following are all fund-based facilities:

1. Demand Loans
2. Term Loans
3. Cash Credits
4. Overdrafts
5. WCDL
6. Advances against Bills
7. Discounting of Future Cash Flows/Rent Receivables and Letter of Credit

2.2 Demand Loan

As the name suggests, such loans are repayable on demand and there is one debit but multiple credits.

Example 5 (Applicable Also for Retail Loans): A customer desires a loan of ₹ 10 lakh for two years to tide over the temporary financial problems in the business against pledge of shares/approved securities/assets created out of the loan.

If the bank is satisfied, a loan will be sanctioned and the amount will be disbursed in one shot and depending on the mutually decided terms of repayment, the loan will be repaid in monthly/ quarterly/half-yearly/annual installment or even full repayment in one lump sum. But there cannot be any second debit/disbursement in the same loan account under same sanction. Loans against term deposits, gold loan, mortgage loan also fall under demand loan category.

2.3 Term Loans

Term loans are for a fixed term and meant for acquisition of fixed assets – land and building, plant and machinery, movable and immovable assets, other infrastructure etc. Unlike demand loans, they are not repayable on demand but only in installments according to terms of repayment.

Example 6: A Transport company wants a loan for ₹ 10 lakhs for purchase of trucks repayable in 60 monthly installments. It would be given by way of term loans where borrower is under obligation for repayment of installments and interest due at the end of each month/quarter as the case may be. Repayment period of term loan is usually 5 to 7 years except infrastructure related areas where repayment extends to longer term.

Appraisal

Appraisal commences with identification and selection of the proponent as it is proper identification that matters.

Appraisal of the credit proposal involves appraisal of:

(a) Acceptability

(b) Assessment of the needs of the customer.

The quality and rigors of appraisal will vary according to the category, type and quantum of loan.

Accordingly, appraisal for clean loans, secured loans, loans to MSMEs, agriculturists and large corporates and firms will vary in depth and dimension.

Identification of the Borrower

A thorough check on the background, experience, competence and dealings in the business (with the customers, suppliers, employees) is essential. Honesty and integrity check should be attached extreme importance.

What Needs to be Done?

In case of corporate borrowers, if the proponent is enjoying banking facilities with other banks, a status report is to be obtained apart from credit score reports from CIBIL (Credit Investigation Bureau of India Ltd.). Status reports are normally given in guarded wordings which may not reveal the real position. Hence, the credit officer must visit the Bank personally and talk to his counterpart of the other Bank to elicit the details of the conduct of the account. The findings should be recorded on the credit file. Reserve Bank of India/Export Credit Guarantee Corporation (if the proponent is also an exporter) publishes list of defaulters periodically. Such information should also be checked.

Managerial Appraisal

Traditionally, bankers are used to making a check on 5 'C's of credit proponent:

(i) Character

(ii) Capital

(iii) Capacity

(iv) Conditions

(v) Collateral

(i) **Character:** Highly subjective. Along with market reports and bankers' reports, personal enquiry by the credit officer is a must. In case of any doubt on this issue, the proposal should not be processed till all doubts are resolved to the satisfaction. Even small loans should not be entertained as the proponent will gain entry to the bank through the small loan and may put the bank in serious difficulties later.

(ii) **Capital:** Financial soundness and solvency of a business is measured by the strength of capital. How far the firm's financial position can deteriorate but still avoid bankruptcy? The answer is in Capital. Hence, bank gives a significant weight age to capital in the process of appraisal. Debt-Equity ratio is one of the salient ratios that Banks give emphasis on, while lending to a project.

(iii) **Capacity:** Capacity of an individual to generate income or a business to generate cash flows so as to make repayments on time is important while appraising a credit application. Capacity includes the efficiency in managing the business of the unit, expertise of the management and staff, future potential, scope of market expansion etc.

(iv) **Conditions:** Economic situation locally and globally (e.g., in times of slump and recession, sales may suffer), firm specific or industry-specific issues, government policies or statutory provisions and such other things affecting consumer demand will also be looked into.

(v) **Collateral:** Collateral is a secondary source of repayment for a bank. Though collateral adds a sense of comfort that in case of default by borrower, bank can fall back upon the collateral security – be it a movable or immovable asset – it is never supposed to be treated as a deciding factor for sanctioning a loan. A credit proposal is always assessed or appraised on the basis of its purpose and ability to generate cash out of the business so as to make repayment and earn profit. While appraising a loan, it is never an intention of the bank to fall back on collateral and close down the business.

The following 5 Cs need to be avoided:

(i) **Cosy:** The appraising authority should not follow a cosy or comfortable approach. In many cases, it is assumed that future will be good because past conduct of the account was good either in the present bank or in the previous bank. There may be instances of strong collaterals, good track record of repayment, or borrower well-known. But under no circumstances, things can be taken for granted. Appraisal should pass through normal/usual checks.

(ii) **Casual:** The officer cannot afford to be 'casual' while obtaining relevant financial and other information, stipulating securities and documents and also appropriate covenants.

(iii) **Clandestine:** Clandestine dealings are strict 'No's. Communication with the proponent needs to be very clear and lack of clarity either oral or written, causes many problems in future. For example, disbursement before perfection of security because of borrower's urgent need on an understanding that security will be perfected at a later date has been a source of major problem in many cases.

(iv) Conformist Approach: At no stage of credit appraisal, conformist approach is tenable. In case any factor comes to the notice of the appraising officer which might give rise to default, it should not be ignored but brought out in the note along with mitigating factors, if any.

(v) Competition: Competition should not drive appraisal. Sometimes, important requirements are diluted because another bank in the vicinity does not insist upon the same. This tendency needs to be avoided. Example: Instead of stipulating equitable mortgage, home loan is sanctioned on the strength of an undertaking to create equitable mortgage as next door competitor lender is doing the same.

2.4 Cash Credits

Unlike demand loans where there is one debit and multiple credits, in cash credit facility, there could be multiple debits and credits. Cash credit (CC) facility is granted mainly to working capital borrowers and upto a limit sanctioned by the bank (sanctioned limit), the borrower can draw and deposit any number of times subject to the sanctioned limit but within permissible drawing limit.

Example 7: M/s Krishna Engineering Works has been sanctioned a CC limit of ₹ 10 lakhs towards working capital facilities at a margin of 25%. This means borrower can draw full limit of ₹ 10 lakhs only when he contributes 25% as his own stake. As the finance is utilized towards working capital, borrower needs to submit statement of stock, periodically, and value of the stock will determine the drawing limits. If value of stock is valued at ₹ 10 lakhs, borrower's margin @ 25% will come to about ₹ 2.5 lakh and borrower can draw only to the extent of ₹ 7.5 lakh even though sanctioned limit is ₹ 10 lakh. If stock statement shows value of stock of ₹ 13.5 lakh or more, then only deducting margin, borrower may draw upto ₹ 10 lakh. However, at no stage, drawing power can exceed sanctioned limit.

Calculation of Drawing Power.

Example 8: **(₹)**

Month	April	May	June	July
Sanctioned Limits	100	100	100	100
Stocks	120	150	180	100
Debtors	90	110	120	80
Total Current Assets	210	260	300	180

Current Liabilities	90	100	80	70
Net Working Capital	120	160	220	110
DP @ 25% margin	90	120	165	82.5
Actual Drawing Limit Set	90	100	100	82.5

2.5 Overdrafts

This facility is usually allowed in current accounts – may be secured or unsecured. Mostly, overdrafts (OD) are allowed on secured basis against liquid securities like Term Deposits, Shares/Debentures, or any other marketable securities. Overdrafts can be availed on a regular basis with a sanctioned limit or on a temporary basis to tide over temporary needs. In overdraft account, like cash credit, there can be multiple credits and debits but unlike cash credit, 'purpose' is not very important. Cash credit facility is necessarily for business purpose and it is important for the bank to be satisfied about the purpose.

Basic requirements for a regular sanction of OD limit are transactions in the current account. Average quarterly balance (AQB) is an indicator for fixation of limit. Some banks have a minimum eligibility criteria of AQB of ₹ 25,000. Existing current account serves the purpose. Unlike cash credit, there is no need of submission of stock statements etc. Interest is computed only for the period the amount is actually drawn.

2.6 Working Capital Demand Loan

In 1995, Reserve Bank of India introduced the loan system of delivery of Bank credit to ensure efficiency in funds management. In this system, the assessed Bank finance is shared between loan and cash credit. Presently, the loan and CC component is decided by the respective bank and the borrower based on the business need. Besides, there might arise sudden temporary need for additional working capital. If bank is satisfied about such immediate need for a short term, a Working Capital Demand Loan can be sanctioned to meet such necessities.

2.7 Advances Against Bills

This is a preferred form of financing of working capital by Banks. Seller may sell either on cash terms or credit terms. If the sale is on cash terms, the bill is known as DP bill (Document against Payment) and if on credit terms, the bill is called DA bill (Document against Acceptance). In case of a DP Bill, the borrower submits the bill consisting of draft drawn by the seller, Railway Receipts or any other transport document, Invoice etc. to his bank and bank upon scrutiny of documents, within sanctioned Bill Purchase limit, will give immediate credit to the borrower's (seller) account usually to the extent of 75% to 80% of the bill amount and balance will be credited after deducting charges, upon payment by the buyer. This is known as Bill Purchase. In case of DA bill, where credit is provided by the seller to the buyer, seller prepares the bill similarly consisting of transport documents, invoice etc. along with Bill of Exchange stating the credit period (30/45/90 days as the case may be) and submits to the bank. Bank will send the bill to buyer's bank. Since buyer enjoys credit period, buyer's bank will deliver the documents including transport receipt only against 'acceptance' of the buyer. Buyer has to accept the bill of exchange drawn by the seller. Upon acceptance, seller's bank may extend finance to the seller within sanctioned Bill Purchase (D/A) limit, again to the extent of 75-80% (depending on the terms of margin). Since in this case consignment passes over to the buyer and Bank has no control on the goods covered by the bill, this is treated clean/unsecured finance. Advance against DA bills is known as Bill Discounting.

2.8 Discounting of Future Cash Flows

Banks also extend financial assistance against future receivables like rent or any such cash flows. Under this scheme, the receivables must be categorically identified. If, for example, future rent receivables are to be discounted, owner's of commercial/residential property having given rent to well- known organizations like Scheduled Banks, Govt. Offices, MNCs may approach the bank for about 70-80% of rent receivables for the period of tenancy less statutory dues, if any.

Interest and other charges will vary from bank to bank and time to time. A tripartite agreement is necessary amongst owner of the property, tenant and the bank.

2.9 Channel Credit

Under this scheme, suppliers to corporates/manufacturing units/distributors etc. are extended financial assistance. This is also known as 'Drawee Bill Finance for Suppliers'. The scheme works as follows:

Example 9:

Supplier : M/s Krishna Engineering Works (KEW)

Buyer : M/s GE Electric

A letter is to be issued by M/s. GE Electric that their past dealings with M/s Krishna Engineering Works (KEW) are satisfactory. Based on the conduct and experience of M/s GE with M/s KEW, Bank would extend a financial assistance (subject to a cap) to M/s. KEW against supplies made to M/s GE for a period usually not exceeding three months. Upon expiry of the period, the amount will be repaid by M/s GE.

2.10 COMMERCIAL PAPER

Commercial Paper (CP) is a money market instrument meant for well-rated corporates to raise short-term borrowings from the market. This is an unsecured promissory note issued for a minimum period of 7 days and maximum of 1 year. The detailed guidelines are given by Reserve Bank of India and can be accessed from master circular issued by RBI – latest one being Master Circular No. RBI/2012-13/99 date 2/7/2012 (www.rbi.org.in). Some features of CP are (Source: Reserve Bank of India):

1. What is Commercial Paper (CP)?

– Commercial Paper (CP) is an unsecured money market instrument issued in the form of a promissory note.

2. When was it introduced?

– It was introduced in India in 1990.

3. Why was it introduced?

– It was introduced in India in 1990 with a view to enabling highly rated corporate borrowers to diversify their sources of short-term borrowings and to provide an additional instrument to investors. Subsequently, primary dealers and all-India financial institutions were also permitted to issue CP to enable them to meet their short-term funding requirements for their operations.

4. Who can issue CP?

– Corporates, primary dealers (PDs) and the All-India Financial Institutions (FIs) are eligible to issue CP.

5. Is there any rating requirement for issuance of CP? And if so, what is the rating requirement?

– Yes. All eligible participants shall obtain the credit rating for issuance of Commercial Paper either from Credit Rating Information Services of India Ltd. (CRISIL) or the Investment Information and Credit Rating Agency of India Ltd. (ICRA) or the Credit Analysis and Research Ltd. (CARE) or the FITCH Ratings India Pvt. Ltd. or such other credit rating agency (CRA) as may be specified by the Reserve Bank of India from time to time, for the purpose.

The minimum credit rating shall be A-2 [As per rating symbol and definition prescribed by Securities and Exchange Board of India (SEBI)].

The issuers shall ensure at the time of issuance of CP that the rating so obtained is current and has not fallen due for review.

6 What is the minimum and maximum period of maturity prescribed for CP?

- CP can be issued for maturities between a minimum of 7 days and a maximum of up to one year from the date of issue. However, the maturity date of the CP should not go beyond the date up to which the credit rating of the issuer is valid.

7. What is the limit up to which a CP can be issued?

- The aggregate amount of CP from an issuer shall be within the limit as approved by its Board of Directors or the quantum indicated by the Credit Rating Agency for the specified rating, whichever is lower.

As regards FIs, they can issue CP within the overall umbrella limit prescribed in the Master Circular on Resource Raising Norms for FIs, issued by DBOD and updated from time to time.

8. In what denominations, a CP that can be issued?

- CP can be issued in denominations of ₹ 5 lakh or multiples thereof.

9. How long can the CP issue remain open?

- The total amount of CP proposed to be issued should be raised within a period of two weeks from the date on which the issuer opens the issue for subscription.

10. Whether CP can be issued on different dates by the same issuer?

- Yes. CP may be issued on a single date or in parts on different dates provided that in the latter case, each CP shall have the same maturity date. Further, every issue of CP, including renewal, shall be treated as a fresh issue.

11. Who can act as Issuing and Paying Agent (IPA)?

- Only a scheduled bank can act as an IPA for issuance of CP.

12. Who can invest in CP?

- Individuals, banking companies, other corporate bodies (registered or incorporated in India) and unincorporated bodies, Non-resident Indians (NRIs) and Foreign Institutional Investors (FIIs) etc. can invest in CPs. However, investment by FIIs would be within the limits set for them by Securities and Exchange Board of India (SEBI) from time-to-time.

13. Whether CP can be held in dematerialized form?

– Yes. CP can be issued either in the form of a promissory note (Schedule I given in the Master Circular – Guidelines for Issue of Commercial Paper dated July 1, 2011 and updated from time to time) or in a dematerialized form through any of the depositories approved by and registered with SEBI. Banks, FIs and PDs can hold CP only in dematerialized form.

14. Whether CP is always issued at a discount?

– Yes. CP will be issued at a discount to face value as may be determined by the issuer.

Example 10: Corporate XYZ wants to issue a CP at an effective rate of 6% for 90 days. What will be the issue price if face value or maturity value is ₹ 100?

$$\text{Issue Price} = \frac{\text{Face Value}}{1 + (\text{Yield} \times \text{No. of Days to Maturity})/365 \times 100}$$

$$= \frac{100}{1.0148}$$

$$= 98.54$$

So, issuer will receive ₹ 98.54 for a CP of ₹ 100.

2.11 Assessment of Working Capital

This is one of the most important areas of credit function. Earlier, Reserve Bank of India had directed Banks to follow certain norms (Tandon-Chore Committee norms) for arriving at maximum admissible Bank Finance but presently Banks are free to determine their own prudential norms for arriving at the amount of working capital. Though the methodology differs from Bank to Bank, Industry to Industry and also on turnover, generally Banks follow two methods:

1. Turnover Method.
2. Maximum Permissible Bank Finance (Method II) based on level of inventory.

1. **Turnover Method:** This method is very simple and is normally applicable to borrowers enjoying fund based and non-fund based limits upto ₹ 5 crores from the Banking System. According to this method, minimum working capital requirement is calculated at 25% of the projected turnover out of which 20% is extended by the Bank and 5% is supposed to be contributed by the borrower as margin. If projected turnover is ₹ 100 borrower has to contribute ₹ 5 and Bank will extend ₹ 20 as working capital finance.

However, projected turnover needs to be carefully looked into, which means turnover projected by the borrower should have a relationship with the past volume and the increase, if any, should be justified with acceptable grounds. The rationale behind 25% of turnover being taken as working capital requirement is based on average production cycle of 3 months which means the borrowers' working capital used for purchase of raw material, blocked in work-in-process, finished goods and receivables come back as cash every 3 months so that this will rotate 4 times a year to achieve the annual turnover. However, some banks, depending on their practice, may follow differential margin.

2. **Maximum Permissible Bank Finance Method:** This method is normally applied by Banks for working capital limits exceeding ₹ 5 crore from the Banking System and the method is in vogue for more than two decades. Particularly, for manufacturing units, level of holding (e.g,. how many months' raw materials, work-in-process, finished goods could be considered for arriving at the need for finance) plays an important role. Though banks are free to decide on the inventory and receivables, generally past history (last 2/3 years), industry norms become an important guide.

Example 11:

	('000)
Projected sale for 2013-14	1,80,000
Raw material consumed per month	7,500
Cost of production per month	10,000
Cost of sales per month	10,000
Stores and spares consumed per month	500
Other current assets	4500
Net Working Capital(Current Assets Less Current Liabilities)	25000

Holding period:

Raw Material	3 months
Stock-in-process	2 months
Finished goods	1½ months
Receivables	1½ months
Stores/Spares	6 months
Credit available on purchase	1 month

(i) Reasonableness of projected sales figure need to be looked into.

(ii) Holding period of above-mentioned current assets need to be verified – bank may follow past practice and also can check from operating statements.

Step 1

Gross Working Capital	:		
Raw Material	: 3 M × 7,500	=	22,500
Stock-in-process	: 2 M × 10,000	=	20,000
Finished Goods	: 1½ M × 10,000	=	15,000
Receivables	: 1½ M × 15,000	=	22,500
Stores/spares	: 6 × 500	=	3,000
Other Current Assets	:	=	4,500
Gross Working Capital			87,500

Step 2

Less: 1 month's credit purchase		7,500
Working Capital Gap	=	80,000

Step 3

Less: 25% of Total current Assets (i.e. ₹.87,500) – ₹ 21,875 or Actual Net Working Capital in the unit ₹ 25,000 whichever is higher

In this case, actual Net working capital available is higher	25,000
So, Maximum Permissible Bank Finance is	55,000

2. Under Turnover Method

Projected Sale	₹ 1,80,000
25% of Projected Sales	₹ 45,000
Less: 5% margin	₹ 9,000
Bank Finance	₹ 36,000

Cash Budget System

Borrowers having working capital limits exceeding ₹ 5 crore from the Banking system has also option to follow cash budget method. But, in such a case, borrowers must have suitable infrastructure to generate required information, MIS as also competent finance professionals. Under this method, borrower needs to generate projected cash budget statement comprising of projected receipts and projected payments. The peak level cash deficit will be the required working capital level to be decided and monitored by the Bank.

A CASE STUDY

Projected Balance Sheet of M/s Krishna Engineering (P) Ltd. as at 31.03.2013

(Amount in ₹ 000)

Liabilities	₹	Assets	₹
Capital	3000	Fixed Assets	5563
General Reserve	700	Advance to employees	248
Profit and Loss A/c	519	Bills and Trade receivables	13058
Term Loan (Bank)	998	Raw Material	6395
Debentures	2000	Stocks-in-Process	2142
Cash Credit (Bank)	11200	Finished goods	3963
Loans from friends and relations	2735	Consumable stores	602
Dues to Directors	803	Advances to suppliers	2276
Fixed Deposits	7028	Deposits with Govt. Depts.	958
Expenses due	415	Profit and Loss A/c	0
Advances received	1023	BG Margin	424
Trade Creditors	5024	Cash and Bank	121
Provision for Tax	305		
Total	35750	Total	35750

The credit analyst has obtained the following additional information on the financial statements of the company:

1. The principal installment of the term loan due within a period of one year is ₹ 10.00 lakh. As on 31.03.13, the entire amount is to be paid.
2. Sister of the Managing Director who is also a guarantor extended a loan to the company @ 10% p.a. interest. The interest is being added to the principal and amounted to ₹ 20.26 lakh as at 31.03.13. The total amount due to the creditor will stand subordinated to the Bank loan.
3. The company incurred losses during the previous years and hence Directors agreed to defer their claims on their unpaid dues till company wipes out the debit balance in the Profit and Loss account. Accordingly, they have agreed to accept payment of the dues from the year 2012-13 in two yearly installments of ₹ 4.00 lakh and ₹ 4.03 lakh respectively.
4. Fixed Deposits received from public include short-term deposits payable within one year to the tune of ₹ 8.45 lakh.

5. Advances made to suppliers include an amount of ₹ 5.00 lakh retained by a supplier as a deposit on a long-term basis.
6. The entire amount of deposits made to government departments represents security deposits against power and telephone connections provided. There is a probability that some current dues are included in the deposits, but the details have not been provided to the Bank.
7. The company is enjoying a Bank guarantee facility at 20% cash margin. Towards the close of the year 31.03.13, a Bank guarantee of ₹ 2.00 lakh is likely to be invoked by the beneficiary with an option for renewal. The company, however, feels that the invocation will be unjust and is not in favour of renewing the guarantee. The company is contemplating to initiate legal action against the beneficiary and has requested the Bank not to pay the invoked amount to the beneficiary.
8. 25% of the advances paid to the employees are short term in nature, recoverable within a maximum period of 11 months.
9. The trade receivables include a total amount of ₹ 11.73 lakh, which is under dispute for last 3 years. The company has accepted responsibility for a discrepancy of ₹ 2.55 lakh in the bills and is ready to forego this amount. For the residual amount, the company contemplates taking legal action against the parties.
10. In course of various inspections, the lending Bank has observed that Consumables include some items purchased five years back, which have been reported at ₹ 0.75 lakh all these three years, but do not have any market value at present.

Apply the information obtained by the credit analyst to the balance sheet figures and restate the current assets, non-current assets, current liabilities and term liabilities. Also comment upon, impact on Net Worth, if any.

Analysis of Balance Sheet

Name: M/s Krishna Engineering (P) Ltd.
Estimates for the year ended/ending 31.03.13

(Amt. in '000)

Particulars	**₹**
Liabilities	
Current Liabilities	
1. Short-term bank borrowing from banks (including Bills purchased, discounted and excess borrowing placed on repayment basis)	11200
Subtotal (A)	11200

2. Short-term borrowing from others	
(i) from friends and relatives	709
(ii) from directors	400
3. Sundry Creditors (trade)	5024
4. Advance payments from customers/deposits dealers	1023
5. Provision for taxation	305
6. Deposits/Installments of term loans/LPGs/debentures etc. (due within one year):	
(i) Fixed deposits due within a year	845
(ii) Term loans due within a year	998
(iii) Expenses due	415
7. Other current liabilities and provisions (due within one year)	
(i) Provision for disputed receivables	255
(ii) Provision for BG invoked	200
Sub Total (B)	10174
8. Total current liabilities	21374
Term Liabilities	
9. Term Deposits (repayable after one year)	6183
10. Other term liabilities (Dues to Directors)	403
11. Debentures not maturing within one year	2000
12. Total Term Liabilities (Total of 9 to 11)	8586
13. Total Outside Liabilities (8 + 12)	29960
Net Worth	
14. Ordinary Share Capital	3000
15. General Reserve	700
16. Other Reserves (excluding provisions/Quasi Equity	2026
17. Surplus (+) or Deficit (–) in Profit and Loss Account	519
(i) Less: Provision for BG invoked	-200
(ii) Less: Provision for disputed bills	-255
(iii) Less: Provision for loss in value of stores	-75
18. Net Worth	5715
19. Total Liabilities (13 + 18)	35675
Assets	
20. Cash and Bank balances	121
21. Receivables other than deferred exports (including bills purchased and discounted by banks)	11885
22. Installments of deferred receivables (due within one year) (Advances to employees)	62

23. Inventory:	
(i) Raw Materials (including stores and other items used in the process of manufacture)	6395
(ii) Stocks-in-process	2142
(iii) Finished goods	3963
(iv) Other consumable spares	527
24. Advances to suppliers of raw materials and stores/spares	1776
25. Other current assets (Margin against BG)	424
26. Total Current Assets	27295
Fixed Assets	
27. Net Block	5563
Other Non-current Assets	
28. Investments/book debts/advances/deposits which are not current assets	
(i) Others (deposit with suppliers)	500
(ii) Advances to employees	186
(iii) Deferred receivables (maturity exceeding one year)	1173
(iv) Others – Disputed receivables deposit with Govt. Departments	958
29. Non-consumable stores and spares	
30. Total Other non-current assets (Total of 28 to 29)	2817
31. Total Assets (Total of 26, 27, 30)	35675
32. Tangible Net Worth	5715
33. Net Working Capital (12 +18) – (27 + 30) to tally with (26 – 8)	5921
34. Current Ratio (items 26 ÷ 8)	1.27
35. Total Outside liabilities/Tangible Net Worth) (13 ÷ 32)	5.24

Working Notes: M/s Krishna Engineering (P) Ltd.

(Respective items in analysis of Balance Sheet have been marked in bracket)

1. Outstanding against Term Loan is to be repaid as on 31.3.2013 as annual installment is ₹ 10 lakh. Hence, the amount of ₹ 9.98 lakh is to be treated as Current Liability [(item 6(ii)].

2. Sister of the M.D. extended a loan to the company which stood subordinated to the Bank loan. This means that company had to undertake not to repay any such loan or interest thereon during currency of the Bank loan. Hence, this might be treated as quasi-equity as this fund would stay in the business as long as Bank loan is outstanding. Hence, the figure of 'Loans from friends and relatives', i.e., ₹ 27.35 lakh will be treated as follows:

Loans from friends and relatives	₹ 27,35,000	
Quasi-equity	₹ 20,26,000	(Item No.16)
Current Liability	₹ 7,09,000	(Item No. 2(i))

3. As on 31.03.2013, debts due to Directors amounting to ₹ 8.03 lakh is to be paid in two annual installments now that the loss is wiped out. Hence, as on 31.03.2013, ₹ 4 lakh is to be paid in one year which is current liability [(Item No. 2(ii)] and balance ₹ 4.03 lakh would be treated as term liability (Item No. 10) being due after one year.
4. Fixed deposits received from public falling due for payment within one year amount to ₹ 8.45 lakh. Hence, this will be current liability [(item 6(i)]. Balance amount (₹ 70.28 lakh less ₹ 8.45 lakh) ₹ 61.83 lakh would be treated as Term Liability [(Item No. 9)].
5. Advances made to suppliers amount to ₹ 22.76 lakh. Since ₹ 5 lakh has been retained as a long term deposit, it will be treated as non-current asset [(Item No. 28(i)]. Rest ₹ 17.76 lakh is to be treated as Current Assets (Item No. 24).
6. Deposits made with government departments ₹ 9.58 lakh by way of power and telephone connections would be non-current assets as these are not likely to be repaid in one year [Item No. 28(iv)].
7. The Bank guarantee invoked is ₹ 2 lakh which the bank is obliged to pay. The amount being in the nature of loss would need to be adjusted from net worth of the company [(Item No. 17(i)]. At the same time, since the amount has to be paid immediately, it would also be treated as Current Liability [(Item No. 7(ii)]. Margin Money (20%) which is provided by the borrower in cash to the Bank amounting to ₹ 4.24 lakh would be treated as Current Assets (Item No. 25).
8. Short-term advances are repayable in one year and hence treated as Current Assets and rests are non-current assets. Therefore, out of ₹ 2.48 lakh, ₹ 0.62 lakh would be treated as current (item No. 22) and ₹ 1.86 lakh Non-current assets [Item No. 28(ii)].
9. ₹ 11.73 lakh represents disputed receivables and as such falls under non-current assets. Hence, out of Trade Receivables of ₹ 130.58 lakh, ₹ 11.73 lakh would be non-current [(Item No. 28(iii)] and ₹ 118.85 lakh as current assets (Item No. 21). To the extent of ₹ 2.55 lakh, company is ready to forego and therefore, would bring down the net worth [(Item No. 17(ii)] as well as reflect as current liability for the same amount [(Item No. 7(i)].

10. Consumables to the extent of ₹ 0.75 lakh have no market value and would be treated by reduction of net worth [Item No.17(iii)].

Calculation of MPBF (Method II)

(Figures in '000)

Total current assets (Item No. 26)	27,295
Less: Other Current Liabilities excluding Bank Borrowings (Total of Item Nos. 2 to 7)	10,174
Working Capital Gap	17,121

This Working Capital Gap less margin would be the level of MPBF. But, margin will be higher of the

(a) 25% of Total Current Assets, i.e., 6,824

or

(b) Net working capital, i.e., current assets less Current liabilities (Item No. 26 Less Item No. 8) 5,921

So, margin here will be 6,824 and MPBF will be computed as:

	17,121
(–)	6,824
MPBF	10,297

Here, we may observe that existing Bank Borrowing is shown as ₹ 11,200 (Item No. 1) and excess Bank Borrowing (₹ 11,200 – ₹ 10,297) of ₹ 903 needs to be brought down.

2.12 CREDIT POLICY

Every bank will have a well laid out credit policy, usually, approved at the Board level. The policy, however, would undergo changes from time to time depending on the market conditions and Bank's risk appetite.

The essence of credit policy is on:

(a) Improvement and maintenance of asset quality.

(b) Focus on priority sector lending including Agriculture, SME and Export Credit.

(c) Financial Inclusion

(d) Improvement of risk-adjusted return and increasing market share

As a matter of fact, aggressive growth, attractive yield and maintenance of asset quality is an impossible trinity. All three cannot be ensured at same time and there has to be a judicious blend of these three factors.

Credit policy covers both fund and non-fund based exposures as well as short-term, medium term and long-term credits.

Credit policy *inter alia*, specifically mentions the importance attached by each bank to different sectors of the economy, e.g., retail loans, loans to SME, export finance, housing sectors, corporate loans, foreign exchange etc. depending on the macroeconomic scenario and banks' risk appetite.

Credit Policy Would Usually Cover

(a) Credit delivery through different delivery channels, e.g., different categories of branches or specialized branches.

(b) Delegation of authority to sanction/approve loan papers at various level.

(c) Types of various facilities like cash credits, working capital demand loan, bill finance, cash management services etc.

(d) Credit thrust like lending to priority sector, financial inclusion etc.

(e) High priority and low priority sectors.

(f) Credit appraisal – various factors to be taken into account.

(g) Assessment of working capital – different methods.

(h) Exposure norms of the Reserve Bank of India and individual Bank's norms. Exposure norms include exposure ceilings for funded, non-funded, single borrower, group borrowers, exposure to capital market, NBFCs, specific industries, specific regions etc.

(i) Security norms – margin and collateral

(j) Various factors determining pricing of products for both fund based and non-fund based.

(k) Various applicable restrictions like Advances against bank's own shares which is prohibited under Banking Regulation Act, 1949, advances to Banks' directors, or relatives of directors.

(l) Risk rating – which would be having a relationship with pricing.

(m) Policies and norms for lending in a consortium arrangement.

Types of Facilities *vis-à-vis* Purpose of Financial Assistance – Some Examples

Type of facility	Purpose of finance
1. Term Loan	Purchase of fixed assets, e.g., acquiring land and building including plant and machinery, constructing shed, housing etc.
2. Demand Loan	Personal loans, Consumer loans, etc.
3. Cash Credit, Acceptance of usance bills	Purchase or holding stock of raw materials, work-in-process, semi-finished goods.
4. Cash credit/Bill Purchase/Bills discounted	Financing receivables.

2.13 Credit Monitoring

Objectives and Functions

Primary objective of credit monitoring is to ensure safety of Banks' funds. As a matter of fact, credit monitoring is equally, if not more important than credit dispensation. In order to ensure safety of funds lent, the following salient points need to be kept in mind.

(a) Credit dispensation shall be subject to laid down procedures. Any deviation should be duly authorized by the competent authority or if circumstances do not permit obtaining approval for reasons of urgency but at the same time deviation is necessary, written remark should be recorded in support of the action, for subsequent ratification/record.

(b) There should be continuous efforts to arrest any slippage and at the same time to upgrade weaker accounts (e.g., substandard to standard).

(c) Close monitoring of performance of assisted units.

(d) Wherever any temporary overdraft, overlimit has been granted, letter of credit devolved or guarantee invoked, close follow-up and monitoring must be done till the irregularities have been regularized.

(e) Inspection of borrowal accounts is often a neglected area. A delinquent borrower takes advantage of banks' laxity in inspection and will jeopardize banks' security.

(f) Timely review of account must be carried out properly and not mechanically.

(g) Restructuring or rehabilitation of accounts, if considered necessary, must be done after due diligence and upon examination of future cash flow.

Tools of Monitoring

1. **Stock/Book Debt Statements:** Applicable for CC accounts. These statements need to be reasonably looked into for deciding the drawing power. The signatory in the statements must be the authorized signatory competent to sign cheques. During inspection of stock, the bank officer should be vigilant about quality and quantity of stocks from a common sense angle and also take out relevant information through inspection of books, interaction with borrowers and their employees.
2. **Audit/Inspection Report:** Audit/Inspection reports are very important sources for monitoring purpose. Some irregularities not noticed by the credit officer may be pointed out by the auditors/RBI or internal inspectors which must be dealt with, with all seriousness.
3. **Scrutiny of the Account:** Conduct of the account is very important. The transactions in the account if scrutinized properly, prove to be very good source of information including diversion, misutilization, reduction in sale etc.
4. **Financial Statements:** Balance sheet, Profit and Loss account – actual and projected.
5. Market reports including **status reports** from other bankers, if any.
6. **Income Tax/Wealth Tax/Sales Tax/Excise Duty,** as applicable on case-to-case basis.
7. **Minutes of the consortium meeting:** Observations made by other members of the consortium based on the position of the account sometimes prove to be important tools of the monitoring.
8. **Comparison of actual performance with projected figures.**
9. **Stock Audit.**

Monitoring is Involved in Three Stages

(a) Prior to disbursement

(b) During disbursement

(c) Post disbursement

Prior to disbursement

A good monitoring in pre-disbursement stage will save the bank time and money and from many hassles post disbursement. Some of the important pre-disbursement monitoring steps are:

(i) **Obtaining status report/market reports:** Status report from other banks and/or market reports from suppliers, customers or those connected with the company should be obtained and, if found necessary, direct interaction is also welcome because sometimes what cannot explicitly be written in report, could be divulged through verbal communication.

(ii) **Pre-disbursement inspection:** Just as before sanction of any credit facility, bank must undertake a thorough pre-sanction inspection, before disbursement also, another inspection is advisable to ensure suitability and readiness of the unit to put funds to proper use. Findings of the inspection and comments of the inspecting officer must be clearly recorded.

(iii) **Acceptance of letter of sanction:** A copy of the letter of sanction, with details of terms and conditions should be obtained duly accepted and acknowledged and it should be preserved as part of other executed documents.

(iv) **Execution of the documents:** Proper documentation is extremely important for the Bank as banks' legal right of recovery depends on appropriate documentation, including stamping wherever necessary. Any lacuna or defect in execution of documents may cause financial loss to the bank as banks' creation of charge over securities/assets may get vitiated. Nature and type of documents will, however, depend on category of borrower (individual, partnership, company etc.) and also nature of facility (Demand Loan, Term Loan, Cash Credit etc.). In view of such importance of documentation, most of the banks have laid down system of getting the documents vetted by legal experts (in-house law officers or outsourced empanelled lawyers).

During Disbursement

The main thrust During disbursement is to ensure proper end use of funds. This can be done in various ways depending on the particular type of loan. Some of the practices followed by banks, are:

(a) To disburse in phases instead of giving the entire funds at a time (e.g., construction of plant/building etc.)

(b) Obtaining consultant's (CA/Architect as the case may be) certificate confirming end-use of funds.

(c) Direct payment to suppliers (e.g., to builders/developers, suppliers of machineries etc.)

(d) Strict compliance of all conditions of sanction.

Post Disbursement

(i) Review on time.

(ii) Obtaining all financials on time.

(iii) Identification of any problem or strain in the account and picking up of early warning signals.

(iv) Identification of warning signals.

Warning Signals which may come to notice within the Bank

(i) Non-compliance of terms of sanction particularly in regard to documentation and security.

(ii) Margin not being contributed from own funds but from borrowed sources.

(iii) Interest not being serviced for more than a week to 10 days after application.

(iv) Installment in arrear for more than a month.

(v) Return of cheque for financial reasons.

(vi) Not routing the entire sale proceeds through the account – a look at the summation of credit entries will throw light.

(vii) Purchased bills not retired on time.

(viii) Continuous utilization of full limit.

(ix) Delay in submission of stock statements without any acceptable reason.

(x) Requests too often for allowing cheques beyond limit or extension of time for repayment of overdrawn funds.

(xi) Letter of credit devolvement/invocation of Bank Guarantee.

(xii) Frequent disruption in functioning of the factory either because of substandard machinery or poor quality of resources including human resources.

(xiii) Production far below the projected level without any plausible reasons.

(xiv) Default in payment of statutory dues.

(xv) Diversion of short-term funds for long-term uses.

(xvi) Sudden spurt in debtors/creditors.

(xvii) Key personnel leaving the organization.

(xviii) Suits being filed against the company by customers/suppliers/employees etc.

(xix) Improper maintenance of records.

(xx) Indifferent outlook of promoters in running the unit.

(xxi) Adverse market report.

Three Most Important Precautionary Measures

(a) Timely Review

(b) Timely Restructuring/Reschedulement

(c) Arrest Slippage

2.14 Trade Finance

Financing trade has been a major activity of banks for a very long time. Trade Finance can be funded as well as non-funded. Banks engage in bill finance – sight bill or usance bill which is in funded category. Under non-funded facility, Letter of Credit and Guarantees are common.

Bill Finance

Under Sight Bill in a trade transaction, seller dispatches goods to buyer by some mode of transport (sea, rail or truck) and in order to retain control over the goods, sends the documents to buyer's bank usually through his bank. The terms of sale can be cash or credit. If the terms of sale are cash, upon dispatch of goods, seller submits the documents comprising among others, Bill of Lading/Railway Receipts/Consignment Notes (as the case may be) accompanied with invoice, bill of exchange, packing list etc. to his Banker with instructions to forward the documents to buyers' bank for collection of payment. At this stage, if the seller already has pre-sanctioned bill finance limit, he may get 75-80% of the bill amount financed by his bank within the limit, balance 15-20% to be considered as margin.

Example 12:

Seller: M/s Krishna Garments (KG)	Buyer: M/s Manosij and Sons (MS)
Location: Mumbai	Location: Kolkata
Dealing in: Garments	Dealing in: Garments
Bankers: Wonderful Bank	Bankers: Excellent Bank
Amount of Sale: ₹ 10,00,000	Amount of Purchase: ₹ 10,00,000

M/s Krishna Garments (KG) has sold garments worth ₹ 10 lakh to M/s. Manosij and Sons (MS) on cash terms. The bill will be drawn as Sight Bill. M/s KG enjoys a pre-sanctioned bill purchase limit (D/P) of ₹ 15,00,000. Margin is 25%.

In this case, M/s Krishna Garments (KG) dispatches the consignment by a reputed transport company and prepares his bill comprising Bill of Exchange,

Transport Receipt, Invoice, List of goods and other documents as applicable and approach his banker 'Wonderful Bank' for purchasing the Bill.

The Bank staff checks the bill and finds papers in order and the amount within sanctioned limit. So, bank will credit the account of M/s KG with ₹ 7,50,000 (75% of the amount of the bill as margin is 25%). Upon purchase, the bill will be sent by Wonderful Bank to M/s Excellent Bank at Kolkata. Since the bill is a sight bill or D/P (Documents against payment) bill, M/s MS has to make immediate payment upon sight of the bill in order to take delivery of the documents. M/s Excellent Bank will collect the amount of the bill (which will include various charges and commissions besides the amount of bill), from M/s MS and release the documents to him to take delivery of goods and remit the proceeds to Wonderful Bank less their charges.

Wonderful Bank, in turn, will deduct the advance amount paid to the seller (M/s KG) earlier and other charges and credit the balance amount. In this case, at all stages, control on goods was retained by the bank till payment was made by the buyer, M/s MS as documents including Transport Receipt were in Bank's custody. The situation would be different if seller would have sold on credit terms. In that case, the bill would have been termed 'D/A' (Documents against acceptance) bill instead of 'D/P'.

In this situation, the buyer's bank (D/A), i.e., Excellent Bank would not demand payment from the buyer M/s. MS before handing over the documents. They would get the bill of exchange accepted by the buyer against his signature, fix the due date depending upon credit period allowed by the seller and release the transport receipt and other documents to the buyer and buyer will take delivery of the goods without making payment (only against 'acceptance' recorded on Bill of Exchange). On the due date, the buyer M/s MS, is supposed to make payment, which will be remitted to Wonderful bank by Excellent bank as before.

In this case, control on the goods is passed on to buyer M/s MS under instruction and responsibility of the seller M/s KG. But if seller's bank purchases the bill, i.e., makes advance payment to seller after the acceptance of the documents by the buyer, M/s MS, the bank is left with no principal security as it looses control over the goods because documents were released by buyer's bank to buyer. Hence, this advance or finance against D/A bill is a clean advance, i.e., without any backing of security except signature as a token of acceptance by M/s MS, the buyer.

That is why, purchasing a D/A bill involves more stringent checks and requires higher authority's approval compared to a D/P bill.

For example, an officer belonging to grade 1 (junior most) has authority to approve purchase of a D/P bill of ₹ 1 lakh. If the bill is D/A, his authority may be reduced to ₹ 40,000 as this will be treated an unsecured (clean) exposure by the bank. Similarly, while granting bill purchase limit to a borrower, if the need is for D/A bill (where seller has to sell on credit terms), bank will adopt more stringent norms (e.g., more collateral etc.) than D/P bill.

Letter of Credit

This is a non-funded facility. Traders avail of this financing facility offered by the banks world over. Under this facility, bank extends financial assistance to seller without any outlay of funds. To define, **a Letter of Credit (LC) is an arrangement between a buyer and his bank to make payment to a third party (seller) a specific amount (value of goods/services supplied) by a specific date in terms with agreed conditions and upon presentation of documents.** Goods are of no significance under LC – only documents matter **(BANKS DEAL ONLY IN DOCUMENTS AND NOT IN GOODS).**

Example 13: Taking out previous Example No. 12, let us assume that M/s KG is dealing with M/s MS for the first time and is not too sure if M/s MS will pay and take delivery of goods after they reach Kolkata. Hence, M/s KG insists on M/s MS to open a Letter of Credit as a pre-condition. The buyer M/s MS agrees and approaches his Bank to open an LC for ₹ 10 lakh in favour of seller M/s KG.

Here also, terms of sale can be cash or credit. If cash, the LC will be a LC – D/P, if on credit, it will be LC – D/A.

Just like in our previous Bill purchase example, the seller's bank needs to sanction a Bill purchase limit to the seller, in this case too, buyer's bank needs to sanction an LC limit to the buyer. Assuming the LC limit is ₹ 15 lakh, buyer's bank would go through the request and upon satisfaction, open the LC in favour of seller. Granting of the LC limit also requires credit check and appraisal of applicant.

Seller M/s KG upon receipt of the LC is supposed to check the terms and conditions thoroughly and, if satisfied, will proceed to make arrangements for production and dispatch of goods. The unique benefit here is that seller need not wait for goods to reach Kolkata or for that matter need not worry if buyer will take delivery of goods. All that seller should worry about is, documents to be submitted to his bank along with the LC are strictly in accordance with stipulations in the LC.

Once the documents are prepared as required by the LC, seller can submit them to this bank and his bank will carefully go through the documents and the LC. If, there is no discrepancy, i.e., documents submitted are strictly in terms of stipulation in the LC, seller's bank will pay the LC amount to the seller which is known as 'Negotiation' (Payment of Value). Seller's bank will claim the amount from the buyer's bank or their correspondent and get reimbursed. Thereafter, the documents will be sent to buyer's bank where they are also supposed to make a thorough check of the documents and if free of discrepancies, would debit the buyer's account and release the documents to the buyer.

Benefits under LC Arrangement

1. There is no need for seller and buyer to know each other.
2. Buyer can place order for the goods or services without any advance payment.
3. Seller would be able to have confidence that he would receive payment immediately on submission of documents post-shipment, if documents are in order.
4. Of course, LC opening bank has to be a bank of repute (prime bank) to command trust of the seller. Otherwise, seller can demand on the buyer to have the LC confirmed by a bank of repute.

Diagramatic Explanation of Various Steps in the Operation of LC

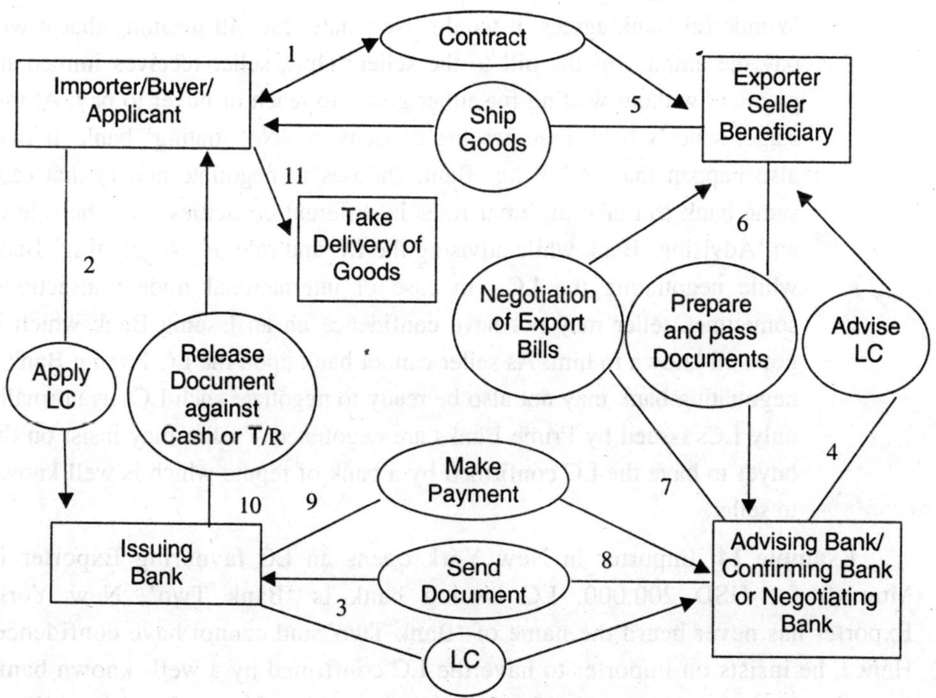

1. Buyer and Seller enters into a deal and seller insists on LC.
2. Buyer approaches his banker and applies for a Letter of Credit (Buyer: Applicant, Buyer's Bank: Issuing Bank)
3. Issuing Bank opens and transmits LC: If Issuing Bank has a branch office in Seller's Centre – LC is usually transmitted through the branch. In the alternative, there would be another bank at the seller's centre with whom Issuing Bank might have already established a correspondent relationship and LC can be advised through the correspondent bank. In our example, 'Excellent Bank' might have established correspondent relationship with another bank, viz., 'Outstanding bank' which has a branch in Mumbai and LC may be transmitted through Outstanding Bank. Outstanding Bank, in this case, becomes 'Advising' Bank and the 'Advising' Bank is responsible only for guaranteeing authenticity of the LC. Advising Bank's role is all the more important in case of International LCs where seller and buyer are in two different countries.
4. Advising Bank advises the LC to seller.
5. Seller goes through the LC, satisfies himself about terms and conditions of LC and ships goods.
6. Upon shipment of goods, seller prepares and submits documents to his bank and if: (a) the documents are discrepancy – free and (b) Sellers' bank, Wonderful Bank agrees, it would 'Negotiate' the bill meaning that it will pay the amount of the bill to the seller. Thus, seller receives immediate payment without waiting for either goods to reach or buyer to pay. At this stage, seller's bank assumes the capacity of 'Negotiating' bank. It may also happen that 'Advising' Bank chooses to negotiate and in that case same bank can take different roles in different capacities (i.e., the role of an 'Advising' Bank while advising the LC and role of 'Negotiating' Bank while negotiating the LC). In case of international trade transactions, sometimes seller may not have confidence on an Issuing Bank which is not well known to him. As seller cannot bank upon the LC Issuing Bank – negotiating bank may not also be ready to negotiate such LCs as normally only LCs issued by Prime Banks are negotiated – seller may insist on the buyer to have the LC confirmed by a bank of repute which is well known to seller.

Example 14: Importer in New York opens an LC favouring Exporter in Mumbai for USD 200,000. LC issuing bank is 'Bank Two', New York. Exporter has never heard the name of 'Bank Two' and cannot have confidence. Hence, he insists on importer to have the LC confirmed by a well- known bank. Importer agrees and requests 'Bank Two' to arrange for confirmation. 'Bank

Two' has a correspondent arrangement with 'Outstanding' Bank which is well reputed MNC Bank, and agrees to confirm upon payment of confirmation charges. Confirming Banks' responsibilities are no less than that of Issuing Bank. While Issuing Bank's responsibility remains, confirming banks' confirmation comforts the beneficiary and negotiating bank with additional responsibility to the extent that, in the event of Issuing Banks' inability to honour the LC commitment, confirming bank will remain liable.

7. Bank agrees to negotiate, check the documents, find them free of discrepancies and makes payment to seller/exporter. This stage is known as 'Negotiation'.
8. Upon negotiation, Negotiating Bank obtains reimbursement from the Reimbursing Bank and sends the documents to the Issuing Bank. Issuing Bank maintains account in the currency of the country of negotiating bank (Nostro Account) with reimbursing bank and instructions were given by the Issuing Bank at the time of opening of the LC to honour the claims of negotiating bank for the amount of LC.
9. In case, the documents were not negotiated by exporter's bank for various reasons like documents were discrepant or exporter/exporter's bank was not willing to have the bills negotiated, documents would be sent to buyer's/importer's bank on collection basis. Under such circumstances, Issuing Bank upon receipt of the documents approach the buyer and, debiting the buyer's account, make payment.

10. to11. Upon receipt of the documents, Issuing Bank makes a thorough check and if they also find the documents discrepancy free, they will debit buyers' account and hand over documents to the buyer. Buyer will surrender the transport receipt to transport company and obtain delivery of goods.

As is observed, we have given emphasis on the issue of documents being non-discrepent. Let us have some discussion on discrepancies. By definition, Letter of Credit mechanism works if documents are strictly in accordance with terms and conditions of Letter of Credit. If any of the documents is not in terms of the stipulations in the LC, it will be a discrepancy. Let us go through the LC given in Annexure V.

It is an LC for USD 350,000/- opened by M/s. MB Pte Ltd. Singapore (Importer) in favour of M/s KB Pvt. Ltd., Mumbai covering shipment of 100% cotton shirts.

Now, let us examine documents [Annexure IV(i)] submitted by the exporter M/s KB Pvt. Ltd. *vis-à-vis* the Letter of Credit (Annexure V).

Draft – Annexure IV(i)

Note the following discrepancies:

(a) Draft is dated March 15, 2013 but the LC expiry date is March 14, 2013.

(b) LC overdrawn by USD 50,000 (LC is issued for USD 350,000 whereas Draft is issued for USD 400,000 (± 5% is allowed under the rules of Uniform Customs and Practices for Documentary Credit 600).

(c) Draft not marked 'Drawn under New Bank of India, Singapore documentary credit No. 23456 issued on January 15, 2013 (as required in the LC).

Invoice – Annexure IV(ii)

1. Invoice indicates merchandise sold to M/s Manosij Bhattacharyya while the buyer's name appearing in the credit is M/s MB Pvt. Ltd.
2. Invoice refers to contract number 1713 whereas LC refers to Purchase Order No. 1703.
3. Size 44 (6000 pieces) shirts are not included in the invoice; trousers are mentioned 3800 pieces of size 36 in the invoice, whereas LC states 4000 pieces and no size.
4. Invoice does not mention that goods are of Indian origin.
5. Invoice signed by Krishna Bhattacharyya instead of seller M/s KB Pvt. Ltd.

Certificate of Origin – Annexure IV(iii)

1. Shows consigned to New Bank of India, Robin Road, Singapore while the credit demands consignee as New Bank of Singapore.
2. Shows consignor as Krishna Bhattacharyya, Ashok Nagar, Kandivli(E) Mumbai 400101 whereas beneficiary is M/s KB Pvt. Ltd., Flat No. 1703, Ashok Nagar, Kandivli (E), Mumbai 400101.
3. Shows purchase order as 1713 instead of 1703 shown in the credit.

Bill of Lading – Annexure IV(iv)

1. Bill of Lading shows notify party as Mr. Jeffrey Chow, 142 Oriol Crescent, Singapore whereas applicants' name is M/s MB Pte Ltd., Flat No. 1406, Katong Park Tower, Singapore.
2. Bill of Lading does not show 'trousers' under description of goods shipped.
3. Bill of Lading shows Freight 'collect' instead of freight prepaid under 'CFR'.

Uniforms Customs and Practices for Documentary Credits (UCPDC)

These are body of rules published by International Chamber of Commerce (ICC) for operation of Letter of Credit mechanism. These rules are revised by ICC from time to time which were first published in 1933 and have undergone six revisions thereafter. Present set of rules is known as UCPDC 600 because they were published in ICC Brochure No. 600 and are in force since 1st July, 2007.

As India is one of the signatories among many countries having agreed to comply with the rules, all banks in India while issuing LCs are required to give an undertaking in the LC, that the LC is subject to UCPDC 600.

(**Example:** "This is subject to Uniform Customs and Practice for Documentary Credits 2007 Revision Publication No. 600").

Besides, ICC had also set up a Documentary Credit Dispute Resolution Expertise (DOCDEX). In case of a dispute concerning any interpretation arising out of a documentary credit, DOCDEX arranges a Dispute Resolution System for Documentary Credit which obviates the need for resorting to expensive legal recourse. Though the decisions of DOCDEX will not be legally binding on the parties, it will surely be a very effective advisory and in case the matter goes to any Court of Law, the decisions of DOCDEX will carry a strong weightage.

Articles

There are 39 articles under UCPDC 600 and 12 articles under e-UCP (which governs presentation of documents in electronic form).

Right from definitions, various parties, documents and the mode of checking of the documents, time limits available for negotiating bank and issuing bank for checking of documents, responsibilities of various parties are contained in these articles. Hence, an Officer posted in export or import department required to deal with Letter of Credit must get conversant with these articles.

Example 15: Exporter M/s KB Pvt. Ltd. submits export documents to their bankers 'Bank Two' for negotiation. 'Bank Two' Bank checks the documents, finds them without any discrepancy, negotiates and pays the amount to beneficiary M/s KB Pvt. Ltd. and obtains reimbursement from issuing bank's Correspondent Bank. Having negotiated, they send the documents to Issuing Bank which is received by Issuing Bank, say on 21st March, 2013. Issuing Bank, however, again is supposed to check the documents with the LC and in course of checking finds that there are two discrepancies which negotiating bank had ignored. Issuing Bank informs these discrepancies on 30th March.

Here, Issuing Bank is at fault under UCPDC – because under article 14(b), the banks have a time limit of maximum five banking days following the day of receipt of documents to arrive at a decision if documents are in compliance with the credit. The documents were received at the office of Issuing Bank on 21st March, 2013. Time available of 5 banking days having expired, Issuing Bank looses its right under UCPDC to claim back the funds.

Immediately, on receipt of advice from Issuing Bank about the discrepancies, Negotiating Bank, even assuming that they agree with the Issuing Bank about the discrepancies which somehow escaped their attention, will take shelter under article 14(b) of UCPDC simply stating that Issuing Bank has pointed out after a lapse of 5 banking days. There will be a staff accountability of the concerned officer at the Issuing Bank.

Example 16: Buyer/Importer lodges complaint with Issuing Bank upon receipt of goods that goods shipped by seller/exporter are totally substandard and do not at all conform to the specifications and description in the LC and requests the bank to take up with exporter's bank.

But under UCPDC Article 5, banks are not at all responsible for the actual goods and services and are responsible only with the documents.

"Banks deal with documents and not with goods, services or performances to which the documents may relate".

Why Would a Buyer Open LC?

LCs are very useful mechanisms for financing of trade. When a buyer and seller are in two distant centres – may be two different countries – and one does not have any knowledge and experience about the other, LCs turn out to be of great advantage between them as bank gives a commitment on payment if the conditions of the LC are complied with. But it is a costly proposition as Bank charges are involved. Some facts are important. If the goods of the seller are in high demand and seller is in a position of strength, he would insist on the buyer for opening of the LC or to send advance payment. Advance payment will be a riskier proposition for the buyer as he does not know seller. Thus, LC suits the buyer. On the contrary, if buyer is in a position of strength by virtue of size, reputation or credibility, he will insist on seller sending goods on open account basis i.e., payment upon receipt of the goods and seller, in order to receive the order from a reputed buyer, will be prepared to send the goods without insisting on LC, on open account basis. In open account transactions, the entire burden of managing risk is taken by the seller. In view of increasing competition and resultant pressure on margins, companies are trying to find out ways of doing business faster and cheaper.

In open account, supplier needs to borrow funds till payment is received from the buyer. Here, large banks who are flush with funds come in the picture. Large banks, especially MNCs, are in a position to make a quick check on buyer's credit risk and based on the risk score, they will pay to the supplier by discounting the bill at some margin over Libor (London Interbank Offer Rate).

Supplier also will reap the benefit of better credit score of the buyer whom he is dealing with by way of lower rate of discount.

With the growth of credit derivative in the international financial markets, the banks discounting the bill are also able to transfer the credit risk through a credit default swap (CDS). CDS is nothing but an insurance instrument against default of the counterparty (buyer in our case). If Seller's Bank discounts the bill of the seller and pays cash, simultaneously it can also buy a CDS from another Bank who against payment of premium depending on buyer's risk score, amount, country and various other factors will insure buyer – risk and guarantee payment in case of buyer's default. Indian Exporters will be able to benefit from these opportunities once CDS market picks up and volume of export goes up. Importance of LCs may come down.

Factoring

Factoring is a well-established means of financing receivables. In factoring, the factor (i.e., the financial institutions) advances money against receivables of the seller (client) to the extent of usually 80% (sometimes even 90%) of the invoice value. Balance amount is paid to the client as and when the full payment is collected. This is a short-term financing – the period being usually 90-150 days (some companies finance even beyond 150 days).

Thus, factoring can be defined as an arrangement for financing a company's business against unpaid invoices drawn in favour of customers and where factor becomes responsible for all credit controls, sales ledger administration and debt collection activities. It is a relationship between the factor (financial institution) and the business entity (the client) selling goods or services to trade customers (the customers) on open account basis where factor purchases client's receivables 'with or without recourse to the client" as well as controls the extended credit and administers the sales ledgers.

Forfaiting

Forfaiting is a mechanism of financing exports.

By discounting export receivables, without recourse to the seller on a discount basis upto full value of contracts with medium to long term maturities.

So, forfaiting is, in essence, a non-recourse discounting of export receivables. The exporter gives up/surrenders, without recourse to him, his rights to claim for payment of goods sold to importer in exchange of cash payment from forfaiter.

As a result, exporter can convert a high value credit sale to a cash sale without any recourse.

Forfaiting is used for international trade transactions with high value sale usually not below USD 100,000.

Factoring	Forfaiting
Usually with recourse	Only without recourse
Continuing transactions	One-time transaction
Mostly consumer goods	Usually capital goods, large projects

Chapter 3

PRIORITY SECTOR LENDING

3.1 Categories of Priority Sector Advances

Lending to Priority sector was conceptualized as far back as July, 1968 at a meeting of National Credit Council deciding on increased involvement of commercial banks in financing of priority sectors – agriculture and small-scale industries. Thereafter, various committees, working groups were constituted to examine and formulate policies on priority sector lending including targets and sub-targets to be achieved by banks. Presently, priority sector for all scheduled commercial banks are categorized broadly as follows:

1. **Agriculture (Direct and Indirect):** Short-term/Medium-term/Long-term loans extended directly to individual farmers, SHGs and others for agriculture and allied activities (dairy, poultry, fishery etc.) come under Direct Agriculture Finance.

   Indirect Agriculture Finance consists of credit facilities for purchase and distribution of fertilizers, pesticides, seeds etc., setting up of agriclinic/Agribusiness centres, construction and running of storage facilities and various other schemes (details of facilities coming under Direct and Indirect Agriculture Finance have been stated in Section 1 of RBI Master Circular No. RBI/2012-13/85 RPCD. Co. RRB. BC No 6/03.05.33/2012-13 dated July, 2013 on Lending to Priority Sector – reproduced in Annexure No. VI.

2. **Micro and Small Enterprises:** Direct Finance: Loans extended to manufacturing enterpri- ses, service enterprises and Khadi and Village

Industries (KVI) Sector are included under this category. Manufacturing Enterprises are again categorized into:

(a) ***Micro (Manufacturing) Enterprises:*** Includes units engaged in production/processing/ preservation of goods subject to the conditions that investment in plant and machinery does not exceed ₹ 25 lakh. Investment means original cost excluding land and building and some items specified by the Ministry of Small-scale Industries vide its notification No. 5.0.1722(E) dated 5/10/2006

(b) ***Small (Manufacturing) Enterprises:*** Same as (a) above except that investment in such units exceeds ₹ 25 lakh but does not exceed ₹ 5 crore. Meaning of investment is also same as (a) above.

3. **Service Enterprises are similarly categorized into:**

(a) ***Micro (Service) Enterprises:*** These are units engaged in rendering of services but with investment in equipments (original cost) excluding cost of land and building, furniture, fittings and any other items not directly related to the service rendered, not exceeding ₹ 10 lakh.

(b) ***Small (Service) Enterprises:*** Same as (a) above except that investment in equipment exceeds ₹ 10 lakh but not ₹ 2 crore. These units will include small road and water transport operators, small business, professional and self-employed persons, various other services like consultancy services, Third Party Administration services for medical insurance claims of policyholders, training centres and educations institutes etc. Loans to micro and small enterprises are classified under priority sector subject, however, to the condition that the enterprises conform to the requirements of being considered as micro and small enterprise under Micro, Small and Medium Enterprises Development Act (MSMED), 2006.

(c) ***Khadi and Village Industries Sector (KVI):*** Loans and advances granted to units in KVI sector are also eligible for being considered under priority sector.

4. **Micro Credit:** Details given in Annexure VII (reproduced from RBI Master Circular No. RBI/2012-13/108 dated 2/7/2012).

Educational Loans

Loans granted to individuals for educational purposes are also eligible for being considered as Priority Sector Advances. (up to ₹ 10 lakh for studies in India and ₹ 20 lakh for studies abroad)

Housing Loans

Loans upto ₹ 25 lakh for construction or purchase of residential units per family (excluding loans sanctioned by Banks to their own employees) as well as loans for repairs upto ₹ 1 lakh in rural areas and ₹ 2 lakh in urban and metropolitan areas are eligible for classification under priority sector.

Weaker Sections

Weaker sections who will be covered under Priority Sector include among others:

1. Small and marginal farmers with land holding of 5 acres and less, and landless labourers, tenant farmers and share croppers.
2. Artisans, village and cottage industries where individual credit limits do not exceed ₹ 50,000.
3. Beneficiaries for Swarnajayanti Gram Swarozgar Yojana (SGSY) now National Rural Livelihood Mission (NRLM).
4. Scheduled Castes and Scheduled Tribes.
5. Beneficiaries of Differential Rate of Interest (DRI) Scheme.
6. Beneficiaries under Swarna Jayanti Sahari Rozgar Yojana (SJSRY).
7. Beneficiaries under the Scheme for Rehabilitation of Manual Scavengers (SRMS).
8. Advances to Self Help Groups (SHGs).
9. Loans to distressed poor to prepay their debt to informal sector, against appropriate collateral or group security.
10. Loans granted under (1) to (9) above to persons from minority communities as may be notified by Government of India from time to time.

3.2 Targets for Priority Sector Advances

Given in Annexure VIII (RBI Master Circular No. RBI/2012-13/108 dated 2nd July, 2012). However, contingent liabilities/off-balance items are not to be classified under priority sector.

Export Credit

Considered under priority sector for foreign banks only.

Common Guidelines for Priority Sector Advances

For all categories of priority sector advances, Reserve Bank of India has prescribed certain guidelines to be followed by banks.

3.3 Application Process

(i) **Application forms:** Bank staff should assist the applicants in completing the forms; however, in case of Government sponsored schemes for weaker sections like SGSY, the relevant project authorities (District Industries Corporation, District Rural Development Agency etc.) may complete the forms.

(ii) **Submission of Applications:** Receipt of applications must be acknowledged by the concerned branch along with a running serial number to be recorded both on the main form as well as the acknowledged portion issued to the applicant. Application form should also contain a 'check list' of necessary papers/documents to be submitted for convenience of applicants.

(iii) **Period of Disposal:**

Amount Applied for	**Disposal time**
Upto credit limit of ₹ 25,000	Fortnight
Over ₹ 25,000	8-9 weeks
Micro and Small Enterprises upto a limit of ₹ 25,000	2 weeks
Micro and Small Enterprises upto a limit of ₹ 5 lakh	4 weeks

(iv) **Rejection of Applications:** Sanctioning authorities may turn down the applications (except SC/ST applicants) on valid grounds but the rejected cases should be verified by the higher authorities subsequently. In case of SC/ST applicants, rejection itself should be done by an authority higher than the sanctioning authority. A proper record with date of receipt, sanction/rejection with reason/disbursement etc. should be maintained for verifications by inspecting officials.

(v) **Disbursement:** Though normally banks prefer to disburse loans directly to suppliers to ensure proper end-use, in case of agricultural purposes, banks are advised to disburse all loans in cash so as to give choice to farmers in selection of dealers. Banks now give an ATM card to enable the farmers to withdraw cash upto permitted drawing limits.

(vi) **Repayment terms:** Repayment schedule should not be fixed mechanically but should take into account the surplus generation capacity, life of the asset, sustenance needs etc. so that practically feasible repayment terms are fixed.

3.4 Financial Inclusion

Inclusive growth and development has been accepted by our policymakers as a necessary phenomenon for more comprehensive growth of our country. The significance of financial inclusion or an inclusive financial system which enables each person to use and take part in the financial system is being emphasized by government, central bank and banking industry. Banks, in particular, have a very important role in implementing the task of financial inclusion. Though, initially this was perceived to be a social obligation, gradually the system has accepted the concept as a business proposition.

What is Financial Inclusion?

As defined by Reserve Bank of India, Financial Inclusion is "the process of ensuring access to appropriate financial products and services needed by all sections of the society in general and vulnerable groups such as weaker sections and low income groups, in particular at an affordable cost, in a fair and transparent manner by regulated, mainstream institutional players".

In essence, financial inclusion is aimed at including the excluded in the formal banking system, provide them savings opportunities and extension of credit so that they can create assets, generate income and improve standard of living. Seven 'A's of Financial Inclusion are: Accessibility, Availability, Affordability, Awareness, Acceptability, Assurance and Appropriateness
(Source: Mr. H.R. Khan, Dy. Governor, RBI).

We have 95000 plus bank branches and about the same number of ATMs. But, still about 60 per cent of adult population does not have a bank account, only 25000 out of 600000 villages in the country have a bank branch.

The data from the following table indicate that we have a long way to achieve the satisfactory level of financial inclusion.

Table: Select Indicators of FI: Cross-country Comparison

Country	No. of Branc hes (per 0.1 million adults)	No. of ATMs (per 0.1 million adults)	Bank loan as per cent of GDP	Bank deposits as per cent of GDP
India	10.64	8.90	51.75	68.43
Australia	29.61	166.92	128.75	107.10
Brazil	46.15	119.63	40.28	53.26
France	41.58	109.80	42.85	34.77
Mexico	14.86	45.77	18.81	22.65
U.S.	35.43	–	46.83	57.78
Korea	18.80	–	90.65	80.82
Philippines	8.07	17.70	21.39	41.93

(*Source*: Report on Trend and Progress of Banking in India, Reserve Bank of India 2011-12)

Engaging Business Correspondents

As establishing physical bank branches in all the unbanked/underbanked centres are not economically viable, RBI, in January 2006, permitted banks to engage business facilitators and business correspondents as a low cost alternative.

It was decided to "enable banks to use the service of NGOs/SHGs, MFIs and other organizations as intermediaries in providing financial and banking services through the use of Business Facilitator and Correspondent Models".

Business Facilitator:

Business Facilitator (BF) ideally is from the village or the area he is supposed to serve and should have knowledge about the livelihood pattern, profile of the farmers and others in the village. Facilitation services include the following besides credit counseling:

(i) Identification of borrowers

(ii) Creating awareness about savings, education and advice on managing money and debt counseling and other products

(iii) Collection, processing and submission of loan applications to banks.

(iv) Preliminary verification of information

(v) Nurturing SHGs/Joint Liability Groups (JLGs)

(vi) Post-sanction monitoring

(vii) Follow-up for recovery

Business Facilitator can be selected by banks from:

(i) Various NGOs

(ii) Post Offices

(iii) Insurance Agents

(iv) Agri Clinics and Agribusiness centres

(v) Cooperative Societies

(vi) Active Panchayats etc.

Business Facilitators, however, are not allowed to handle cash transactions.

Eligibility criteria for engaging Business facilitators are as follows:

Individuals:

(a) Permanent resident of the area

(b) Minimum educational qualification of the level of S.S.C. pass

(c) Age: 21 to 50 years (flexible)

(d) Should be attached to only one Bank

(e) No criminal proceeding in any court of law

(f) Should not have been a defaulter to any bank

Institutional:

(a) Office-bearers/promoters should have a satisfactory track record

(b) Neither the institution nor its office-bearer should be defaulters to any bank

(c) Must be attached to only one bank

(d) In case of a registered organization, there should be specific authority to work as Business Facilitator and latest balance sheet to be looked into.

Business Correspondent Model

The very basic concept of Business Correspondent model evolved out of the necessity to cover each village in the country under organized financial service. As only about 27% of rural households were found to have access to financial services, it was very difficult to bring the rest 70% plus within the fold. The hurdles in increasing access to finance were mainly cost of delivery through brick and mortar bank branches as well as cost to customers. So, 'Business Correspondent' model was the right answer and in 2006 Reserve Bank of India came out with its circular allowing use of business correspondents for expanding the coverage.

As is the case with BF, BC's role is also like an intermediary between bank and the customer. In addition to the functions performed by BF, BC is also authorized to transact cash on behalf of the branch.

Persons and Organizations Who can be Enlisted as Business Correspondents:

(a) NGOs

(b) Companies registered u/s 25 of the Companies Act, 1956

(c) MFIs set up under Trust Acts

(d) Registered Societies

(e) Insurance Agents

(f) Post offices

(g) KVC

(h) Retired Bank employees/Govt. employees

(i) Ex-servicemen

Functions of BCs:

(a) Mobilization of small deposits

(b) Disbursement of small loans

(c) Recovery and collection of principal and interest

(d) Sale of third party products

(e) Handling remittances of small value

As the banking business is carried out on behalf of the bank but away from banks' branches, it involves significant reputation and operational risks for the respective banks. Therefore, Banks impose limits on cash holding by BC, individual receipts/payments by BCs as well as make sure that whatever transactions are undertaken by a BC on a single day gets reflected in the Banks' books of accounts earliest possible, not later than next day.

Eligibility Norms for Selection of BCs:

Usually, BCs are institutions.

(a) NGOs/MFIs/Societies/Companies incorporated u/s 25 of Companies Act, 1956.

(b) Registered NBFC not engaged in accepting Public Deposits. (Objective clause of the registered entities should specifically contain authority to act as BC).

(c) Good track record of the office bearers.

(d) Institutions or its office-bearers must not be a defaulter to any bank/financial institution.

(e) For registered institutions, latest balance sheets to be looked into. Like in BFs, retired bank/government employees/ex-servicemen can also be appointed as BCs.

Modus Operandi

BCs are selected by the appropriate authority of the bank in terms of laid down Guidelines.

About 5-6 BCs are attached to a branch. Each BC caters to about 5-6 villages within a radius of 15-20 km area of operation. BC is given a handheld device and the villager/customer a smart card which enables recording of the transaction (deposit/withdrawal) through biometric process. The device with the BC is also voice enabled in local language to satisfy the customer about the authenticity of the transaction as well as to serve blind/illiterate customers. Each BC is allowed an overdraft limit ranging usually from ₹ 10000 to ₹ 50000 depending upon the comfort level of the bank, collateral offered etc. Transaction limit per BC per day is, however, set by the bank and minimum amount (₹ 10 usually)/maximum amount of withdrawal is also set.

At the end of the day, BC needs to upload the transaction to the Bank server and settle the net of cash received/paid with the branch.

BC is usually paid a combined revenue – fixed and variable component. A fixed amount of about ₹ 3000 is paid for initial settling expenses followed by variable payment depending on value/volume of transactions handled.

RBI Governor, Dr. D. Subbarao in a speech on 4th March, 2013 said "Financial inclusion is a necessary condition for sustaining economic growth..... Financial inclusion is good for all the stakeholders.

(a) **Good for the poor:** Opportunity to improve their income and their quality of life.

(b) **Good for the banks:** Steady low cost savings – Asset Liability Management.

(c) **Good for the government:** Powerful tool of poverty reduction, it also cuts down leakage.

(d) **Good for the economy:** Savings of the poor into the formal financial sector.

Win-win for the poor, banks, government and economy. Not just a public good but a merit good".

Growth and Progress in Financial Inclusion is shown in Annexure IX (Source: PPT of Ms. Deepali Pant Joshi of RBI).

Annexure XXII also gives progress under financial inclusion plan as also microfinance program (Source: Report on Trends and Progress of Banking in India 2011-12).

Chapter 4

NON-PERFORMING ASSETS

4.1 Non-Performing Assets

What is a Non-performing Asset?

An asset, including a leased asset, becomes non-performing when it ceases to generate income for the bank.

A non-performing asset (NPA) is a loan or an advance where:

(i) Interest and/or installment of principal remains overdue for a period of more than 90 days in respect of a term loan.

(ii) The account remains 'out of order', in respect of an Overdraft/Cash Credit (OD/CC) for more than 90 days.

(iii) The bill remains overdue for a period of more than 90 days in the case of bills purchased and discounted.

(iv) The installment of principal or interest thereon remains overdue for two crop seasons for short duration crops in Agricultural advance.

(v) The installment of principal or interest thereon remains overdue for one crop season for long duration crops in Agricultural advance.

(vi) The amount of liquidity facility remains outstanding for more than 90 days, in respect of a securitization transaction undertaken in terms of guidelines on securitization dated February 1, 2006.

(vii) In respect of derivative transactions, the overdue receivables representing positive mark-to-market value of a derivative contract, if these remain unpaid for a period of 90 days from the specified due date for payment.

What is an 'Out of Order' Status?

An account is termed 'Out of Order' if the balance outstanding in the account is in excess of sanctioned limit or drawing limit.

Example 17: C/C account with a limit of ₹ 1,00,000 margin 20%. At the end of a quarter, stock statement submitted by the borrower shows value of stock ₹ 1,00,000.

The account will show:

Sanctioned Limit : ₹ 1,00,000

Drawing Limit : ₹ 80,000 (20% margin)

In such a position if the debit outstanding in the account is in excess of ₹ 80,000, the account will be classified as 'Out of Order', even though sanctioned limit is ₹ 1,00,000. If stock statement shows value of stock as ₹ 1,25,000 the sanctioned limit and drawing limit will both be ₹ 1,00,000. But if outstanding is in excess of ₹ 1,00,000, the account will surely be termed Out of Order.

Example 18: Again, the outstanding balance may be well within the sanctioned/drawing limit but there is no credit entry in the account continuously for 90 days.

A/c : M/s ABC

Sanctioned Limit : ₹ 5,00,000

Drawing Limit : ₹ 5,00,000

Date	Debit	Credit	Balance
01/12/12	B/F		Dr. 4,00,000
27/12/12	Interest charged 12,000		Dr. 4,12,000
28/12/12	Self 50,000		Dr. 4,62,000

As at 31st March, 2013, if there is no credit in the account, the account will be treated as NPA inspite of the fact that the outstanding is well within the sanctioned and drawing limit.

If any amount under any credit facility is not paid on due date, it will be treated 'Overdue'.

4.2 Income Recognition

In tune with International norms, Banks are not to recognize any interest on NPA account as income. Thus, income is to be recognized only on realization basis, not on accrual basis. Exception: Interest on loans against deposits, NSCs, Life policies etc. provided sufficient margin is available. If a loan of ₹ 75,000 is granted against a Fixed Deposit of ₹ 1,00,000, interest charged in loan account may be recognized as income even if there is no credit in the account.

Asset Classification

Non-performing Assets are classified into the following three categories:

1. Substandard Assets
2. Doubtful Assets
3. Loss Assets

1. **Substandard Assets:** We have seen that an account becomes NPA if interest is not serviced/account remains out of order for continuous period of 90 days. From the time it becomes NPA, it will be categorized as Substandard for a period upto 12 months.
2. **Doubtful Assets:** If the asset remains in Substandard category for a further period of 12 months, it is categorized as Doubtful Assets. An asset can remain in the Doubtful category maximum for 36 months after which the asset will be classified as 'Loss' assets.

   However, it is not that an asset needs to travel the entire route to be qualified as 'Loss' assets. Bank can categorize an asset as a 'Loss' one even without journey through prior categorization, provided in the opinion of the Bank or RBI, the asset has no salvage value or insignificant (less than 10%) salvage value.
3. **Loss Assets:** If the asset is identified as loss to the bank without any salvage value or insignificant (usually less than 10%) salvage value by the bank, internal or external auditors or RBI inspectors and that the asset is not recoverable, it is categorized as Loss Asset.

Classification of Asset is Borrower-wise Not Facility-wise

If a borrower has more than one facility with a Bank and any one facility becomes NPA, all the other facilities though not NPA will be classified as such because the borrower will be classified as NPA.

Example 19: A Borrower has the following facilities with the Bank:

Bill Purchase

Cash Credit

Term Loan

Interest on Term Loan is overdue exceeding 90 days and has been an NPA. The other accounts Cash Credit and Bill Purchase, though in order, will also be NPA as the borrower will be NPA.

Consortium Arrangement

In a consortium arrangement, a borrower enjoys advance facilities from more than one bank. In such cases, classification is done on the basis of record of recovery of individual member banks.

Example 20: Borrower having facilities from:

Wonderful Bank : Lead Bank

Excellent Bank : Member

Outstanding Bank : Member

If the remittances from borrower are deposited with Wonderful Bank and shares of Excellent and Outstanding Bank are not transferred leading to the account being NPA with them, the account will be NPA with Excellent and Outstanding Bank and not with Wonderful Bank.

Agricultural Advances

If interest or principal in an agricultural loan account for short duration crops remains overdue for two crop seasons, the account will be treated NPA. But if the loan account is for long duration crops, the account will be NPA provided overdue remains for one crop season. Long duration crops are crops requiring more than one year upto harvesting. Crop season is as decided in the respective State by the State Level Bankers' Committee.

Government Guaranteed Advances

Any advances if guaranteed by Central Government, will not be treated NPA upon being overdue or out of order for 90 days as in other cases, but on the following event:

Guarantee invoked by the bank but repudiated by the government. In case, the guarantor, i.e., the Central Government does not honour its guarantee for any reason, when called upon to pay because of overdue, NPA classification will hold good. But in case of State Government guaranteed advances, if overdue exceed 90 days period, the account will be treated NPA.

4.3 Provisioning Norms

Prudential norms require Banks to make appropriate provisions against assets.

Standard Assets

Requirement for general provisions for standard assets on balance outstanding are as under:

(a) Direct agricultural advance and Small and Micro Enterprises Sector @ 0.25%.

(b) Commercial Real Estate Sector @ 1%.

(c) Housing loans if granted at teaser rates (i.e., rates which are low to start with compared to market rate and entice borrowers to avail of the loan but are increased gradually after a certain period – also known as Adjustable rate mortgage), will attract provisions at 2% but would come down to 0.4% after expiry of 1 year from the date the normal, i.e., higher rate is reset, provided, however, the asset is not an NPA.

Restructured Advances

Any restructured account which is categorized as standard assets will be subject to 2% provision during first two years from the date of restructuring. In case a moratorium on payment of principal/interest is allowed, provision requirement will be 2% during the moratorium period and two years thereafter.

If a restructured account is classified as NPA and subsequently upgraded to standard category, 2% provisions required will be for the first year from the date of upgradation.

Substandard Assets

Unsecured exposures – 25% on the outstanding balance.

Secured exposures – 15% without any allowance for available securities or ECGC cover.

Doubtful Assets

(a) Portion of outstanding which is not covered by the realizable value of securities (value to be estimated by the bank on a realistic basis) – 100%

(b) Portion of outstanding which is covered by securities will be subject to provision as follows depending on the age of the asset remaining doubtful.

Doubtful upto one year	:	25%
Doubtful one to three years	:	40%
Doubtful for three years	:	100%

Loss Assets

Loss assets usually are required to be written off. In case, Bank decides to carry the loss assets in the books, required provision is 100% of the outstanding.

Provision Coverage Ratio

This is a ratio of total provisions to gross NPAs. In effect, this means the amount of funds bank has reserved to guard against losses arising out of problem loans. Provisions add to the soundness of the bank and financial system. RBI has decided that total provisions in a Bank, i.e., provisions arising out of prudential norms as applicable to various classes of NPAs plus floating provisions should be strengthened so as to ensure a provision coverage ratio of (PCR) 70% and PCR should be disclosed in the notes to accounts of the Balance Sheet.

Example 21: Provision required to be made for accounts guaranteed by ECGC.

An SME account guaranteed by ECGC has become NPA and is in the Doubtful Category – Doubtful for 2 years 6 months.

Outstanding balance	:	₹ 2 lakh
ECGC cover	:	50%
Value of security held by the Bank	:	₹ 0.5 lakh

How much provision is required to be made?

Solution:

Outstanding Balance	:	₹ 2 lakh
Less: Value of Security	:	₹ 0.5 lakh
Unrealized balance	:	₹ 1.5 lakh
Less: ECGC cover (50% of unrealized balance)	:	₹ 0.75 lakh
Net unsecured balance	:	₹ 0.75 lakh
Provision for unsecured portion	:	₹ 0.75 lakh (100%)
Provision for secured portion	:	₹ 0.20 lakh (40% of Secured portion)
Total provision required	:	₹ 0.95 lakh

Annex-X (RBI Master Circular No. RBI/2012-13/39 dated July 2, 2012) for computation of NPA.

NPA Management

Various costs of holding an NPA in Bank's books:

Direct Costs

(a) Cessation of interest income

(b) Gradual increase of provision out of current income

(c) Cost of holding the asset – funding cost as well as cost of maintenance of the asset

(d) Cost of capital

(e) Cost of recovery

(f) Loss of income due to blockage of funds and inability to recycle/redeploy funds for income generation

(g) Deterioration in value of security

Indirect Costs

(a) Adverse market perception and consequent impact, in stock market, Bank's credibility goes down.

(b) Further credit expansion also slows down.

4.4 Reasons for NPA

Reasons attributed to the borrowal account:

Internal

(a) Willful default

(b) Managerial incompetence

(c) Financial indiscipline

(d) Internal dispute among partners/co-promoters/unhealthy labour relations

(e) Technological obsolescence

(f) Faulty Machinery causing substandard products

(g) Inventory pile up

(h) Delay in receivable collection

(i) High Staff Turnover

(j) Diversion/Siphoning of funds

External

(a) Economic slowdown and depressed market.

(b) Changes in government policies

(c) Strikes and riots

(d) Poor loan repayment environments due to wrong publicity by vested interest group

(e) Shortage of inputs

(f) Infrastructural deficiency

Reasons Attributed to Bank

(a) Wrong identification of the borrower

(b) Poor pre-sanction appraisal – absence of physical verification of security where applicable

(c) Inadequate and deficient information on borrower and industry

(d) Over-reliance on past satisfactory relation with the borrower ignoring the economic viability

(e) Mechanical routine approach while reviewing an existing account.

(f) Improper repayment schedule

(g) Misutilization of loans

(h) Lack of communication with borrowers

(i) Imperfect documentation

(j) Failure to pick up warning signals

Points to Remember for Retaining Asset Quality

(a) Recover the overdue through active follow-up.

(b) In case of problems arising out of temporary cash flow mismatches, do not stop transactions in the account; instead allow 'holding on' operation.

('Holding on' operation: Allowing a portion of every deposit to be utilized towards outstanding and balance allowed to be withdrawn. Otherwise, borrower is likely to have clandestine operations with other bank keeping existing account as NPA).

(c) Discuss with the borrower threadbare about expected cash flows, examine the basis of receipt of cash flows and thereafter reschedule the terms of repayment or restructure the debts, by allowing moratorium, if warranted.

Preventive Steps for Accounts under 'Watch' Category

(a) Compliance of terms of sanction.

(b) Strict and close monitoring – written and oral reminders.

(c) Any overdue to be recovered earliest to avoid slippage.

(d) Close supervision and inspection of security charged to the bank.

(e) In terms of respective Banks' restructuring policy, reschedulement/ restructuring can be done, if necessary to avoid the account slipping into NPA.

Some Common Action Points for Bringing Down NPA

(a) At the first sign of problems, default, stress, close monitoring to be commenced.

(b) Irregularities about accounts mentioned in Audit report (Internal Audit/RBI Audit/Statutory Audit) to be dealt with in all seriousness and regularized.

(c) Stock statements/stock inspection, wherever applicable, should be ensured on time and with seriousness attached.

(d) Financial statements submitted by the borrower should be looked into thoroughly and analyzed. Annual Review should be carried out without delay.

(e) Strict vigil on securities – periodic valuation to be carried out.

(f) Asset classification to be correctly done.

(g) Intense efforts for upgradation of assets and recovery in accounts earlier written off.

4.5 Tools of NPA Management

(a) Recovery Camps: Periodic setting up of camps at a place within the area of operation of the branch which acts as an impetus on the defaulting borrowers.

(b) Lok Adalat: Under Legal Services Authority Act, 1987, bank branches arrange organizing Lok Adalats with the help of District/Subdivision Legal Services Committee. It is an important Alternative Dispute Resolution mechanism. Banks prefer this mode of recovery for small dues as on-the-spot settlement is done. Disposal of cases are simple, quick and cost-effective.

(c) Debt Recovery Tribunals: Debt Recovery Tribunals were established under the provisions of 'The Recovery of Debt Due to Banks and Financial Institutions Act, 1993' mainly with the object of recovery of problem loans faster as prior to passage of this Act, large number of such cases filed by Banks in civil courts were pending for years. Debt Recovery Tribunals are located across the country having defined territorial jurisdiction. These Tribunals are presided by a presiding officer of the rank of District and Sessions Judge and assisted by Recovery Officers. Cases in excess of ₹ 10 lakh (or ₹ 1 lakh where Central Government so decides for certain types of debts) come under the purview of Debt Recovery Tribunals. Though initially these were welcome by the Banking sector with the hope of expeditious recovery and bringing down NPAs significantly, it was observed that settlement, decree and realization of dues consumed time as legal processes were involved. This experience led to the passage of SARFAESI Act, 2002.

(d) **SARFAESI Act:** Action under Securitization and Reconstruction of Financial Assets and Enforcement of Security Interest Act (SARFAESI), 2002 has been a significant development over other legal measures inasmuch as banks can, without the intervention of Court, sell the charged properties by giving a 60 day's notice.

Agricultural land does not come under purview of SARFAESI Act. Banks, under this Act, can attach the property upon expiry of 60 day's period and subsequently go for sale. In case, there is no response from any bidder for purchase above the reserve price, the lender can buy the property. Through the Banking Amendment Bill, 2012, Banks and Asset Reconstruction companies are empowered to convert the debt into equity. However, Banks are not interested to take over the asset as it is not the business of the Bank but this Act has given teeth to the lenders to use more as a threat than actual taking over and selling the asset. For example, a bank has financed ₹ 1 crore for a large poultry farm and the account has been an NPA. If Bank takes over the asset, it will be an added burden on the bank to manage the poultry including live birds till a satisfactory purchaser is located.

Once bank issues 60-day notice, most of the borrowers come forward for settlement which is the underlying purpose.

(e) **Compromise:** This is also an effective mode of recovery. If bank has reason to believe that the borrower is not a willful defaulter and is not in a position to revive the business or the position does not warrant a rehabilitation/reschedulement/restructuring, the bank can discuss and negotiate for a compromise where bank will sacrifice a part of the loan dues (may be penal interest, interest etc. depending upon the position of the borrower, security available etc.) and accept balance amount in full and final payment of the loan.

Sale of NPA to Asset Recovery Companies

Concept of sale of problem assets to Asset Reconstruction companies is of recent origin. There are now quite a few such companies in India like M/s ARCIL (Asset Reconstruction Company of India Ltd.), M/s ASREC (India) Ltd., M/s ISARC (India SME Asset Reconstruction Company Ltd.), M/s Edelweiss Asset Reconstruction Company Ltd., etc.

In this business, the first step is to acquire non-performing loans from the lender, after the price discovery is agreed to between both sides which is a difficult process. Asset Reconstruction in India owes its origin to Narasimhan Committee I which conceived the idea of setting up an Asset Reconstruction Fund. This was not implemented. Narasimhan Committee II laid down the recommen- dation of ARC in line with international experience. The objective of ARCs was not only to acquire the bad loans from the lenders with the aim of optimal recovery and management, but also to reconstruct the bad loans with good ones.

Recovery Agent/Enforcement Agents

Where recovery is not forthcoming, the Bank may explore the avenue of engaging the services of Recovery Agents. These include Government Agencies, NGOs, SHGs, Corporate Bodies/Firms and trained individuals with proven track record.

Continuous and constant contact and follow-up with the borrower is the best tool. Being in contact with the borrower will give a clearer picture about the financial position, future potential of the business as well as facilitate taking a decision on nursing of the unit. If temporary cash flow is perceived to be the problem, nursing is the best solution and appropriate reschedulement is necessary. But if the condition of the borrower is beyond revival and the borrower is willing to settle the dues with some concession, Bank should discuss and enter into a compromise settlement. If the borrower appears to be recalcitrant and unwilling to pay but securities are available, notice under SARFAESI Act, can be issued.

It is to be kept in mind that legal action is always a last resort. If nothing is workable and securities are also not available, bank would have no other alternative but to write off. **But efforts to recover must continue even in written off accounts as such amounts recovered will enhance the profit straightaway.**

4.6 Dealing with an NPA Account

A credit officer might resort to the following flow chart in tackling an NPA account:

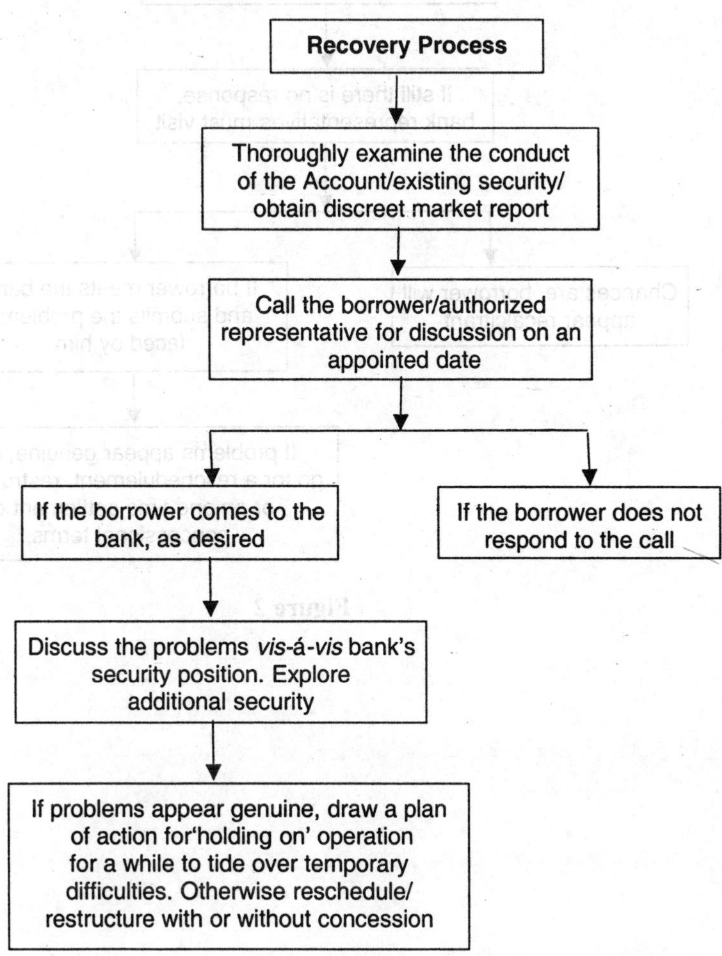

Figure 1

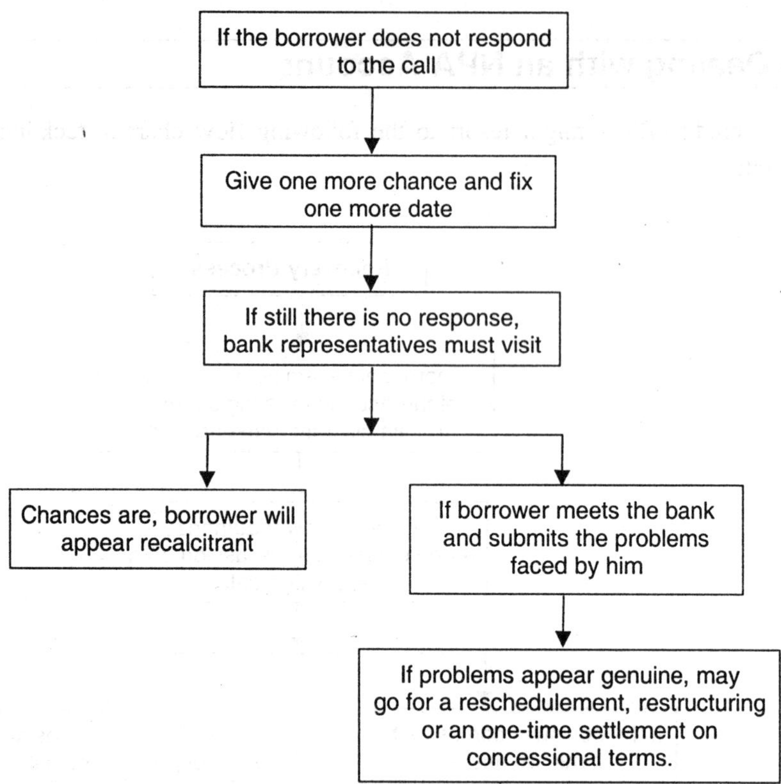
If the borrower does not respond to the call
Give one more chance and fix one more date
If still there is no response, bank representatives must visit
Chances are, borrower will appear recalcitrant
If borrower meets the bank and submits the problems faced by him
If problems appear genuine, may go for a reschedulement, restructuring or an one-time settlement on concessional terms.

Figure 2

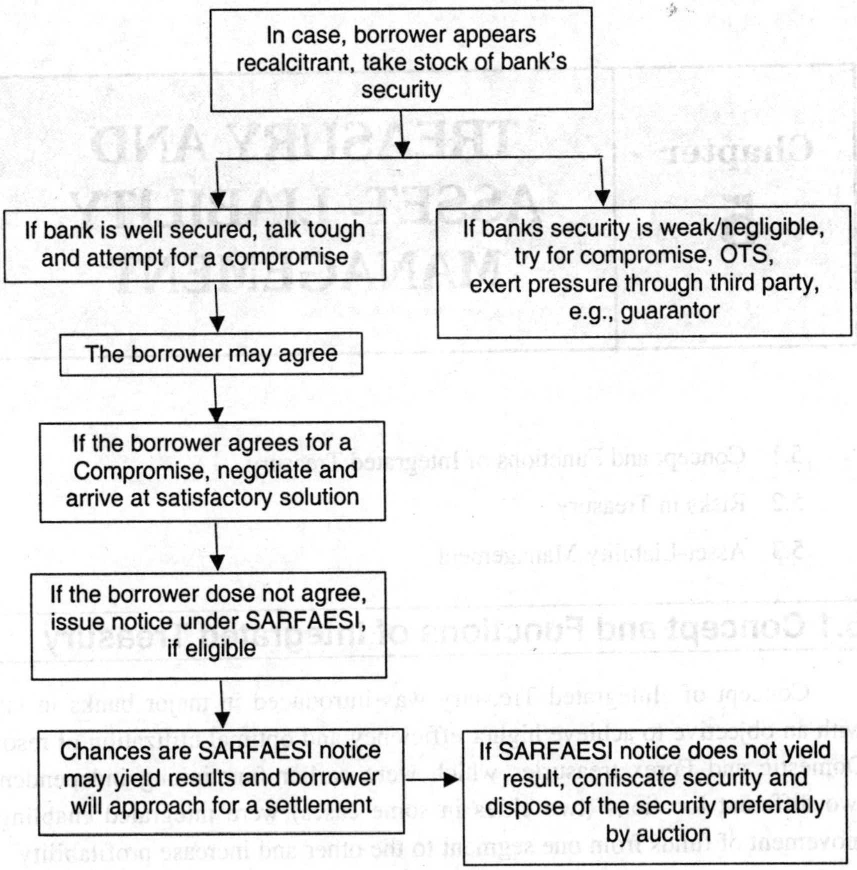

In case, borrower appears recalcitrant, take stock of bank's security

If bank is well secured, talk tough and attempt for a compromise

If banks security is weak/negligible, try for compromise, OTS, exert pressure through third party, e.g., guarantor

The borrower may agree

If the borrower agrees for a Compromise, negotiate and arrive at satisfactory solution

If the borrower dose not agree, issue notice under SARFAESI, if eligible

Chances are SARFAESI notice may yield results and borrower will approach for a settlement

If SARFAESI notice does not yield result, confiscate security and dispose of the security preferably by auction

Figure 3

Annexure XXIV shows composition of NPAs of public sector banks for 10 years.

Chapter 5

TREASURY AND ASSET- LIABILITY MANAGEMENT

5.1 Concept and Functions of Integrated Treasury

Concept of Integrated Treasury was introduced in major banks in late 90s with an objective to achieve higher efficiency and optimal utilization of resources. Domestic and Forex treasuries which were earlier functioning independently at two different locations (two cities in some cases) were integrated enabling easy movement of funds from one segment to the other and increase profitability.

Important Functions of Integrated Treasury:

- Management of Funds
- Pricing of Products – Announcing Base Rate
- Maintenance of statutory requirements:
  - (a) Cash Reserve Ratio
  - (b) Statutory Liquidity Ratio
- Foreign Exchange operations
- Investments – analyzing money market and maximizing returns through trading.
- Asset-Liability Management
- Controlling market risk
- Compliance of Regulatory Requirement
- Nostro Reconciliation

Broadly, however, Treasury Division of a Bank has three functional segments:

1. **Front Office:**

    (a) ***Dealing Foreign Exchange, Merchant and Interbank:*** Here, dealers buy, sell, borrow or lend currencies/securities through screen-based trading. Depending on the size and volume of business of a bank, it will have number of dealers, both in money market and foreign exchange market. One bank may have one dealer in one currency or one dealer for various currencies or more than one dealer for one currency.

    (b) ***Money Market:*** Funds Management, Cash Reserve Ratio

    (c) ***Fixed Income:*** SLR (Statutory Liquidity Ratio) and Non-SLR Management

    (d) ***Equity:*** IPOs and Secondary market

    (e) ***Derivatives:*** Trading for customers

2. **Back Office:**

    (i) Accounting

    (ii) Confirmations

    (iii) Contracts

    (iv) Settlements

    (v) Funds Management

    Keeps a check on Front Office transactions and is engaged in accounting and settlement of transactions carried out by Front Office. As a measure of prudence, back office and front office are supposed to be completely separate from each other.

3. **Mid Office – Risk Management:** Monitoring of limits – Daylight, overnight, stop loss, Bank Exposures, Gaps, VaR, Evaluation of Profit.

    (i) Review of policies on various limits

    (ii) Monitor derivatives

    (iii) Management of risks including on FCNR-B portfolio

    (iv) Review of Brokers

Management of Funds being one of the most significant job of Treasury, involves three parameters:

(a) Safety

(b) Liquidity

(c) Return

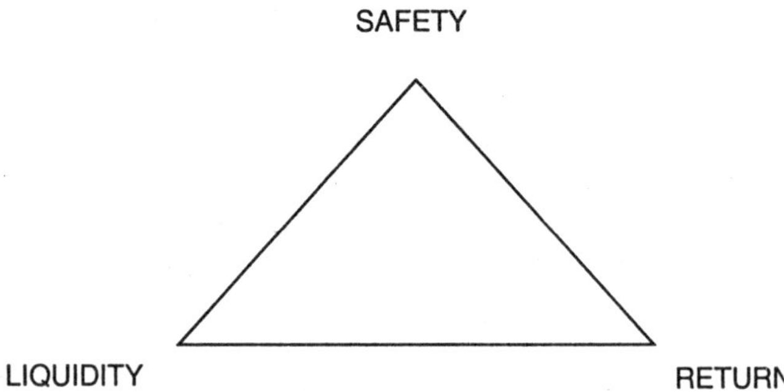

It is a difficult job to strike a balance amongst these three parameters.

Fund managers always aim at optimizing the yield keeping an eye on liquidity and risk profile. As we know, usually longer the maturity, higher the yield but it is also true that, higher the yield, higher the risk.

Cost of Liabilities

Fund Managers are primarily concerned with actual cost of funds as well as effective yield.

Example 22: A Depositor approaches the Bank with an offer to deposit ₹ 5 crore for 1 year and desires a loan of the same amount for same maturity at 0.50% spread. Deposit rate for 1 year for the amount is 7% p.a. How would you react? (Assume: CRR – 4% p. a., SLR – 23% p. a., 1-year G-Sec Yield – 7.8% p. a.)

In order to decide if the offer is acceptable, it is necessary to arrive at actual cost of fund.

On a deposit of ₹ 100,

(a) Interest cost – ₹ 7.

(b) CRR requirement presently is 4% (₹ 4) on which Bank does not earn anything.

(c) SLR requirement presently is 23% (₹ 23).

(d) Yield on the SLR corresponding to 1 year G-Sec @ 7.8% p.a. is ₹ 1.794 (₹ 23 × 7.8%).

(e) Interest yield on ₹ 27 (CRR + SLR) = ₹ 1.794.

(f) Balance left for deployment is ₹ 73 (₹ 100 – ₹ 27).

(g) Cost of ₹ 73 available for deployment is (₹ 7, Interest cost) – (1.794, yield on SLR) = ₹ 5.206.

(h) Cost of deposits (₹ 5.206/₹ 73) % = 7.13%.

This is without taking into account compounding of interest rates and reinvestment of yield on SLR.

Under the circumstances, spread in the current proposal of 0.50% gets reduced to 37 basis points, i.e., 0.37% which after taking into account operating expenses and other costs may not become viable.

Based on the market and yield on deployment, risk profile and maturity, treasury manager moves fund from one market to another. Fund manager keeps a strict vigil on the market movements – be it forex, money or derivatives to take arbitrage benefits.

Sources of Profits in Treasury Operations:

(a) Forex market operations:

- Both merchant and proprietary
- Arbitrage in different markets
- Cash and derivative segments

(b) Money Market (A market for short-term funds not exceeding one year):

- Churning of securities
- Borrowing/Lending funds
- Retailing of Government securities

(c) Segments of money market:

- Call money (overnight), Notice money (2-14 days), Term money (exceeding 14 days), Treasury Bill, Commercial Paper, Certificate of Deposit, Repo and Reverse Repo, Bill Discounting.
- Securities market comprises of government securities (G-Sec) and other securities approved for SLR compliance.
- Corporate Debt-Non-SLR securities, Debentures, Bonds – convertible, floating and fixed rate, callable, zero coupon etc.

(d) Investments from/in overseas market:

- Investments by FII
- ADR/GDR issues of Indian corporates
- Exchange Earners' Foreign currency
- Foreign currency funds of Banks etc.

5.2 Risks in Treasury

Treasury operations involve mainly market risk but credit/counter party and operational risks are also present. In debt, equity and forex transactions counterparty risks exist.

Market risks comprise of liquidity risk and interest rate risk which exist to a large extent in treasury operations for which Asset-Liability Management (ALM) is very crucial.

Operational risk arises out of the nature of activities/operations.

Various Risk Management measures like Dual control, Internal control including exposure ceiling limits, position limits, deal size limits, open position limits, stop loss limits are put in place.

Risk Measurement

Some important, commonly practiced risk measurement measures include Value at Risk (VaR), Duration, Gap analysis etc. which we will explain in the following section on Asset-Liability Management.

Derivatives

Derivatives are used by market makers, hedgers, speculators, arbitragers. Basic derivatives are forwards, futures, options and swaps.

5.3 Asset-Liability Management

ALM in India has gained importance as a result of changing scenario of Indian Banking System. It was not important when interest rates were fixed and governed by Central Bank of the country and Banks functioned in a regulated market with assured interest margins. There was no threat to survival. Gradually, we have seen deregulation in interest rates across all segments, banks functioning with increasing freedom, integration of domestic and global markets with a feeling of threat to survival. Banks mainly faced the following challenges:

(a) Risk Management

(b) Return on Capital

(c) Balance between Risk and Return

The following factors necessitated strengthening ALM mechanism:

(a) Financial volatility as a result of increase in cross-border transaction and increasing deregulations

(b) New financial products – this will increase with the improvement of financial market

(c) Regulatory initiatives

(d) Increasing awareness of top management

Aims and Objectives of ALM

Objective of ALM is not to eliminate risk but to manage. Broadly, the objective of ALM is to control the volatility of Net Interest Income (NII),[1] liquidity risk and ensure a balance between profitability and growth.

Thus, ALM mainly attempts to control market risk which is a function of:

(a) Interest Rate Risk

(b) Price Risk

ALM also aims at Balance Sheet management and management of Liquidity Risk.

ALM process comprises of:

(a) **ALM information system:** A strong MIS – availability, adequacy and accuracy of information.

(b) **ALM organization:** Involvement of top management with efficient structure and responsibilities.

A first comprehensive guideline was issued by Reserve Bank of India in February 1999 (Annexure XI). Modifications as and when necessary was done subsequently. In terms of RBI Guidelines, ALCO (Asset Liability Committee) consisting of senior management and headed by CEO/CMD or next in seniority is the highest decision-making body responsible for balance sheet planning from risk-return perspective. The Committee meets on fortnightly basis. ALCO is primarily responsible for interest risk management and for co-ordination of bank's strategies to achieve optimal risk/reward trade-off.

Some important common terminologies used in ALM:

(i) Time buckets

(ii) Inflows and outflows

(iii) Residual maturity

(iv) Rate-sensitive Assets (RSA)

(v) Rate-sensitive Liabilities (RSL)

(vi) Gap method

(vii) Duration

(viii) M-Duration

(i) **Time Buckets:** In terms of present RBI guidelines, all assets and liabilities are to be grouped as per their maturity profile into 10 maturity buckets as follows:

---

[1] NII is Interest Income Minus Interest Expenditure.

- Day 1
- 2-7 days
- 8-14 days
- 15-28 days
- 29 days to 3 months
- Over 3 months to 6 months
- Over 6 months to 12 months
- Over 1 year to 2 years
- Over 2 years to 5 years
- Over 5 years

(ii) **Inflows and Outflows:** All inflows and outflows of funds pertaining to the particular time bucket are to be grouped and gap determined.

Example 23: A bank makes a ₹ 5 lakh vehicle loan to a borrower to be repaid lumpsum on 4th year at a rate of 10% p.a. This loan is funded initially by a one year fixed deposit of ₹ 5 lakh at a rate of 6% p.a. Bank's Margin is 4%. Where is the risk?

Bank should go for a Gap analysis. Gap is Assets minus Liabilities. In this example, deposit being for one year, will be placed in 6 months to 1 year time bucket under outflows whereas Assets will be grouped in 2-5 years under inflows. So, 6 months to 1 year time bucket will show 0 (inflow) minus 5 lakh (outflow) resulting in a negative gap of ₹ 5 lakh. Even though, Bank's lending was with a spread of 4% (10% minus 6%), at the end of 1 year when bank has to repay the deposit and borrow further ₹ 5 lakh to fund the asset, spread will fall if there is a rise in interest rate.

(iii) **Residual Maturity:** It refers to the balance time which a particular asset or liability will take to mature. If a Gap is being calculated in July 2013 between a five year term deposit for which 4 years have elapsed and a 5 year term loan for which only 1 year has elapsed, residual maturity for the term deposit will be 1 year and placed in that relevant time bucket whereas the term loan will have residual maturity of 4 year and placed in the time bucket of 3 to 5 years.

(iv) **Rate-sensitive Asset (RSA):** Assets that are subject to changes in rate and include those assets which will mature in a specified time period.

(v) **Rate-sensitive Liabilities (RSL):** Liabilities which are subject to changes in rate and includes those that will mature in a specified time period.

Example: Current Account balances are not included in RSL as they are not sensitive to rates.

An assets or liability is considered rate sensitive if during the time period:

(a) It matures or can be repriced

(b) It represents full or part payment

(vi) **GAP Method:** Gap = Inflows minus Outflows (bucket wise)

Inflow > Outflow = Positive Gap

Inflow < Outflow = Negative Gap

(vii) **Duration:** Duration is a measure of price volatility. It is the weighted average maturity of assets/liabilities/off-balance sheet items where present values of all cash flows are used as weights. In effect, Duration is a measure of actual maturity that takes into account timing and size of a security's cash flows.

(viii) **Measure of Duration is in Units of Time:** A simple example of Duration is given in a Table below:

Security of ₹ 100 maturing in 5 years with a coupon rate of 10% p.a.

Year (A)	**Coupon (B) ₹**	**PV (C) ₹**	**Weight (A × C) (D)**
1	10	9.09	9.09
2	10	8.26	16.52
3	10	7.51	22.53
4	10	6.83	27.32
5	110	68.30	341.50
Total		99.99 Say 100	416.96

Duration = 416.96/100 = 4.17 years

Column A – Year

Column B – Coupon (Interest Amount)

Column C – PV = Present Value of coupon. Since ₹ 10 will be paid at the end of the year, present value of ₹ 10 is 10/(1 + .1) = ₹ 9.09

Assume interest rate is lower @ 8% p.a. for the same security.

PV (C)	Weights (D)
9.26	9.26
8.57	17.14
7.94	23.82
7.35	29.40
73.50	367.50
106.62	447.12

Duration – 447.12/106.62 = 4.19

With lower rate, Duration has increased.

Interest rate is higher at 12% p.a. for the same security.

PV (C)	Weights (D)
8.93	8.93
7.97	15.94
7.12	21.36
6.35	25.40
63.55	317.75
93.92	389.38

Duration – 389.38/93.92 = 4.15

With higher interest rate, Duration has decreased.

M-Duration

Modified duration is a measurement of interest rate sensitivity which means if there is 1% change in market yield, the consequent % change in the price of security. M-Duration is arrived at dividing Duration by (1 + YTM%)[2]. If M-Duration is 3, it means 1% change in the current market yield will cause 3% change in the price of security. Duration is measured in units of time whereas M-duration is in terms of % of price.

[2] YTM is yield to maturity which is the overall return on the bond if the same is held till maturity.

In our previous examples, Duration was 4.17 years and YTM is 10%. So, M-Duration is 4.17/1 + .1 = 3.79%.

Similarly, in the other example of coupon rate of 8% p.a. Duration was 4.19. M-Duration would be 4.19/1 + .08 = 3.88%.

Common Ways of Risk Redressal

1. **Liquidity Risk:**

   (a) Construct maturity ladder and calculate cumulative surplus/deficit of funds (mismatch) at selected time period (Annexure XII).

   (b) Tolerance level limit (e.g., 20% of cash outflows).

   (c) Short-term dynamic liquidity statement for 1-90 days (Annexure XIII).

2. **Currency Risk:** Value at Risk (VaR) approach and set tolerance limit.

3. **Value at Risk (VaR):** This denotes the maximum amount of money which bank may lose on a portfolio over a given level of confidence and specified period of time. It is a statistical measure and VaR result shows, for example, maximum possible loss in, say, in a day with 95% confidence level which means probability of loss exceeding the level is only 5%.

4. **Interest Rate Risk:**

   - Gap reports by grouping risk-sensitive Assets/Liabilities and off-balance sheet exposures with the use of maturity buckets.

   - Bank to take a view on Net Interest Margin taking into account likely interest rate movements. In short, interest rate risk is the likely loss from unexpected movement in interest rates which adversely affects bank's profitability and market value of equity. So, interest rate risk (IRR) surfaces whenever income of the bank is sensitive to interest rate changes.

Techniques mentioned earlier like Duration/M-Duration, Gap Analysis, VaR are commonly used to measure IRR. Sometimes, simulation is also used when future business volumes are analyzed under various alternative interest rate possibilities.

Example 24:

Assets and Liabilities as on 31-12-13 of Wonderful Bank

Liabilities	Position as on 31/12/13	Assets	Position as on 31/12/13
Capital	500	Cash	60
Reserves and Surplus	1250	Balances with RBI	1500
Demand Deposits	7850	Balances with other Banks	700
Time Deposits	9150	Investments	4000
Borrowings	350	Advances	14000
Other Liabilities	1570	Fixed Assets Other Assets	250 160
Total Liabilities	20670	Total Assets	20670

The following are assumptions:

1. Outstanding under LC and Bank Guarantees are ₹ 1250 crore and ₹ 750 crore respectively. Past-behavioral analysis reflects that 5% of these non-funded exposures would get crystallized into fund-based exposures because of devolvement/invocation.
2. The bank has placed committed lines of credit to other banks to the extent of ₹ 100 crores out of which ₹ 50 crore are unutilized.
3. Non-performing Assets included in the Total Advances are ₹ 250 crore.

Let us prepare a Structural Liquidity Gap report. The Annexure No. XII shows:

In the 1-3 year bucket, outflows are more than inflows resulting a negative gap where mismatches exceed outflows substantially.

Changes in Net Interest Income (NII) is related to the Gap size (Annexure XIV, XV and XVI).

Δ NII = Gap $\times$ Δ Interest

Specimen agenda/deliberations on issues in ALCO Meeting:

Example 25:

1. Confirmation of Minutes (Meeting dated ....).
2. Short-term dynamic liquidity statement for the fortnight dated ......
3. Market scenario
4. Structural liquidity/interest rate sensitivity for the period ....
5. Money market transactions as on ....
6. Position of CRR/SLR, interbank liabilities (related to net worth).

❋ ❋ ❋

Chapter 6 FOREIGN EXCHANGE BASICS

6.1 Concept of Exchange Rate

Foreign Exchange means exchange of one currency in terms of another. Hence, just like exchange of commodities at a price, two currencies are also traded at a rate of exchange at a particular point in time which lies at the core of exchange rate mechanism. Since the market of foreign exchange is open 24 hours at some centre or other in the globe and the volume is very high, the rate changes very first (approx. 15-20 times a minute on an average) which causes potential for profit/loss in the trade. Some commonly accepted terminologies of the market are:

1. **Bid rate:** The rate at which the market is prepared to purchase a currency.
2. **Ask rate:** Also known as offer rate. It is the rate at which the market is prepared to sell a currency.

   For obvious reasons, when a two way rate is quoted (e.g., U.S. $ 1 = INR 61.50 – 61.60), the lower one would be buying rate and the higher one would be selling rate, as any rational business entity will buy a commodity at a lower rate and sale at a higher rate, the difference being profit margin.

   But this concept applies to countries which follow the practice of direct rate. India now follows direct rate. Earlier, in India till July, 1993, indirect rate was being followed (e.g., ₹ 100 = U.S. $ 2.5350 – 2.5550) where home currency was fixed and traders followed the principle of 'buy high, sell low' meaning buy more of a commodity and sell less of the same commodity difference being the margin of profit.

3. **Base Currency:** Since two currencies are involved, in order to avoid confusion, one is taken as base currency. Any transaction is quoted from base currency perspective. Mr. X telephones his bank about USD/INR rate. The Bank replies: U.S. $1 = ₹ 61.50/60. This means, bank would buy USD at ₹ 61.50 and sell at ₹ 61.60. This is known as two-way quotation.

   U.S. $ here is the base currency, as U.S. $ is being bought and sold.

4. **Value Date:** The date on which actual delivery of currency takes place.

5. **Spot:** Type of transaction where value date is 2 business days following the day of transaction.

   Example 26: Bank 'X' enters into a spot purchase of U.S. $ 100,000 @ ₹ 61.50 with Bank 'Y' on 7th June 2013 which is a Friday. Amount/Rate/Date of delivery is all decided on 7th June, 2013. Only actual delivery will take place on 11th June, 2013 (Tuesday) (Saturday and Sunday being closed). On 11th June 2013, Bank X's nostro account (USD A/c in USA) will be credited with U.S. $ 100,000 and Indian Rupee account with Reserve Bank of India will be debited with ₹ 61,50,000 and Bank Y's Indian Rupee account will be credited with equivalent rupees and nostro account debited.

   Similarly, value can be cash/Tom/Forward. In case of value cash, delivery and transaction would take place on the same date, i.e., 7th June, 2013 and for value Tom (tomorrow), delivery and transaction both take place on Monday, i.e., 10th June, 2013. Delivery taking place any day beyond 11th is known as Forward Transaction.

6. **Cross Rate**

   Example 27: When rates for a particular pair of currency are not available in one market, the rate is obtained indirectly by crossing rate of one of the currencies from another market.

   Mumbai – USD 1 = ₹ 61.50 – 60

   London – GBP 1 = USD 1.56 – 57

   At what rate can an importer buy £ against INR?

   Solution: Bank will sell USD against INR at ₹ 61.60 (bank will charge higher of the two) and overseas market will sell GBP @ USD 1.57 (also higher of the two). So, rate applicable for buying GBP is 1.57 × 61.60 = INR 96.72

   Example 28: Exchange rates in Mumbai Market and London Market are as follows:

Mumbai Market

USD1 = 61.25 – 61.28

Overseas Market

USD1 = SGD 1.3202 – 1.3302

At what rate one can buy SGD against rupee?

Solution: Mumbai Bank will buy USD @ ₹ 61.28 as market will sell U.S. Dollar at the higher rate. This U.S. Dollar will be taken to overseas market and buy Singapore Dollar @ 1.3202 as market will give at the lower rate. So, applicable rates for this transaction are:

USD/INR = U.S. \$ 1 = ₹ 61.28

USD/SGD = U.S. \$ 1 = SGD 1.3202

Now, the solution is just a simple arithmetic:

If U.S. \$ 1 = ₹ 61.28 = SGD 1.3202

SGD 1.3202 = ₹ 61.28

$$\text{SGD} = 1\ \frac{61.28}{1.3202} = 46.42$$

Example 29: An importer wants to remit AUD 50,000 when rates quoted are as under:

Mumbai – U.S. \$ 1= ₹ 61.25/61.28 and USD/AUD in foreign market is quoted as U.S. \$1 = A \$ 1.3900/1.3910.

If a margin of 0.15% is to be loaded in the exchange rate, calculate rate to be quoted and rupee amount to be paid by the importer.

Solution: Since AUD is to be sold against Rupee, we need cross rate. We need to buy AUD against USD and USD against INR. USD-INR in our case would be 61.28 and USD/AUD would be 1.3900.

USD 1	=	A \$ 1.3900
USD 1	=	61.28
A \$ 1	=	44.09
Add: 0.15%	=	07
		44.16

Thus, total Rupee amount to be paid by the importer is A \$ 50,000 × 44.16 = ₹ 22,08,000.00

USD is at a premium because you need more rupees to buy USD 1 after 1 month.

In a system of Direct Rate, premium is added to buying and selling rate. Similarly, discount is deducted from buying and selling rate in a Direct Rate system.

Example 33: Interbank Rate

Spot USD/INR = ₹ 61.50/55

One month forward points = 16/17

Solution: The thumb rule is if right hand figure of forward points is higher than left hand figure (i.e., ascending order), the base currency is in premium. Hence, the forward differentials will be added to the spot rate to arrive at one month forward rate, which will be ₹ 61.66/72.

Factors responsible for forward differentials:

1. **Interest Rate differentials**: A very important factor causing forward differentials of two currencies where both the countries are having full convertibility, i.e., current and capital account convertibility. At present, India does not have capital account convertibility and hence capital flows are not free from restrictions. As a result, interest rate differential between India and USA (in case of USD/INR) would not be a prime factor for forward differential of USD/INR.
2. **Demand and supply for the currency for the forward date:** If we are looking at 1 month forward rate for USD/INR and there happens to be greater number of buyers than sellers for 1 month delivery, the differential will push up based on law of demand. Similarly, suppliers exceeding buyers will drive the differential down.

6.3 Forward contracts – Some issues

Early Delivery

It is not necessary that the customer will always deliver the currency on due date. He may deliver earlier than agreed.

In such cases, banks do take or give delivery of foreign currencies earlier than agreed date but this will necessitate for the bank to enter with additional interbank deals to rectify the situation arising out of the action of the customer. A swap transaction follows: 'Swap' means buying or selling the same currency for different value dates. It may be spot/forward or forward/forward.

Spot/Forward means:
Buy spot/sell forward OR
Sell spot/buy forward

Forward/Forward means:

Buy forward (e.g., 1 month)/Sell forward (e.g., 3 months) OR

Sell forward (e.g., 1 month)/Buy forwards (e.g., 3 months)

Example 34: On January 1, your bank had entered into a forward contract for U.S. $ 100,000 with an exporter, delivery June 30. The customer approached the bank on April 15, with delivery of the currency as he has received payment earlier. Bank's position will be as follows:

January 1: While entering into the contract with the customer on January 1 to buy U.S. $ 100,000 on June 30, bank simultaneously entered into another contract in the market to sell the currency on June 30.

So, on January 1, i.e., the day of booking the contract, banks position book will show:

	U.S. $	U.S. $
June 30	+ 100,000 bought	– 100,000 Sold

(This is known as square position.)

On April 15, the customer approaches the bank with early delivery. Bank's position undergoes change as follows:

April 15	June 30
+ U.S. $ 100,000	– U.S. $ 100,000
(overbought)	(oversold)

So, bank will sell spot with value April 15 and buy forward value June 30. This is a case of Swap. In this transaction, in all probability, there will be loss or gain depending on the currency being at a premium/discount which, for obvious reasons, will be on customer's account.

Example 35: Bank XXX agreed to purchase USD 100,000 delivery on May 31. The contract rate was USD 1 = ₹ 62.00. On March 1, the customer approached the bank with the delivery of the currency amounting to USD 100,000 which was supposed to be delivered on May 31.

How would the bank deal with the situation?

Interbank rates on March 1:

Spot USD 1 = ₹ 61.25 – ₹ 61.28

Forwards	= March	2200 – 2400
	April	3500 – 3800
	May	5050 – 5450

Solution: This is a case of early delivery and hence necessitates a swap.

Bank would purchase USD 100,000 delivered on March 1 and would sell spot in the market. While booking the contract delivery on May 31, bank would have committed to sell in the market on May 31 for which the bank has to buy forward value on May 31.

Bank will sell spot at the market buying rate @ ₹ 61.25 and buy for May 31 @ market selling rate.

Spot USD 1	61.2800 (Market selling rate)
Plus Premium	.5450
	61.8250

Amount sold spot @ 61.25	= ₹ 61,25,000
Amount required for buying @ 61.8250	= ₹ 61,82,500

So, swap loss is ₹ 57,500/- which customer has to bear.

Further:

1. Original amount at the contract rate of USD 1 = ₹ 62 comes to ₹ 62,00,000.
2. Amount at the Spot selling rate of USD 1 = ₹ 61.25 comes to ₹ 61,25,000.

Bank would have received more by ₹ 75,000 at the contracted rate which is deemed to be the cash outlay for the bank. Interest for March to May, i.e., 3 months @ 9% (base rate) comes to ₹ 1,687 plus banks charges – say ₹ 1,000. Thus, customer has to bear –

₹ 57,500 + ₹ 1,687 + ₹ 1,000 = ₹ 60187.

It may so happen that for some reasons (Government policy, and dispute with the buyer or for any other reasons), the obligation under the contract is not honored at all by the customer. Under the circumstances, the customer has to make the request in writing to his bank and the bank would recover/pay the difference between the contracted rate and the rate at which the contract is cancelled.

Applicable Rates

1. Purchase contracts shall be cancelled at the banks' spot TT selling rate prevailing on the day of cancellation.
2. Sale contracts shall be cancelled at the banks' TT buying rate prevailing on the day of cancellation.
3. If the contract is required to be cancelled before the date of maturity, the applicable rate will be corresponding forward TT rate.

4. In case there is no news from the customer even after maturity of the contract, the contract shall automatically be cancelled on the 7th working day after maturity. Saturday is excluded from calculation of working days.

   In case of cancellation after due date, the customer will not receive any exchange difference, should there be any in his favour, whereas any difference against him is obviously on his account.

Example 36: Bank XXX booked a forward purchase contract for USD 100,000/- delivery January 31, at USD 1 = ₹ 62. On the delivery date, i.e., January 31, the customer approaches the bank to cancel the contract. Rates quoted in the market are as follows:

Spot USD 1 = ₹ 62.55 – 62.58

Exchange margin: 0 -1% on TT (Buying) Rate and .22% on TT (Selling) Rate

Cancellation of a purchase contract is effected at the bank's spot TT selling rate. What is the TT selling rate on January 31?

Solution:

Spot USD 1	₹ 62.55 – 58
Spot selling rate	62.5800
Add: Exchange margin @ .22%	.1377
	62.7177

USD 1 = ₹ 62.72

How much will be payable by customer?

Under the purchase contract, customer was to receive (USD 100,000 @ ₹ 62) ₹ 62,00,000

Upon cancellation customer has to pay USD 100,000 @ ₹ 62.72 = ₹ 62,72,000. The difference comes to ₹ 72,000 plus cancellation charges.

Cover Operations

Foreign exchange transactions result in two types of positions – Exchange Position and Cash Position. All purchases and sales – Spot and Forward – are included in the Exchange position.

Cash position includes only the transaction that affects the nostro account balance either by credit or debit.

Example 37: Forward purchase contract of U.S. $ 50,000 is booked on Feb 1, 2013 for delivery on April 1, 2013

Exchange position on Feb. 1, 2013: + U.S. $ 50,000

Cash position on April 1, 2013: + U.S. $ 50,000 (assuming delivery takes place on April 1)

A Bank may be overbought (long) or oversold (short) in a currency. Overbought (long) position indicates that Bank has ended up purchasing or agreeing to purchase more than it has sold or agreed to sale in that particular currency. Similarly, oversold (short) position indicates that the bank has ended up selling or agreeing to sale more than it has purchased or agreed to purchase in that particular currency. If a bank is neither overbought not oversold meaning that it has purchased a currency equal to what it has sold, then the position is known as square.

At the end of a trading day, a bank may have an overbought position which it likes to square up. It may do the same by a spot sale or a forward sale in that currency in the interbank market. Similarly, oversold position can be squared up by a spot purchase or forward purchase in that currency.

Example 38:

Date: 01/02/13

Opening Exchange Position USD 10,000 overbought

Opening Cash Position USD 1,05,000

Transactions:

1. Booked forward purchase contract USD 50,000
2. Purchased export bill 45 days' usance USD 25,000
3. Issued a DD USD 30,000

If you are required to maintain a Cash Position of USD 20,000 and stay square in exchange position, what would be the right transaction?

Solution:

Currency U.S. $

Exchange Position	Purchase	Sales	Net Position
Opening Position			10000 (O/B)
Forward Purchase	50000		
Purchase of Export Bill	25000		85000 (O/B)
Issue of DD		30000	55000 (O/B)
Cash Position	Cr.	Dr.	Balance
Opening Balance			Cr. 1,05,000
Issue of DD		30000	Cr. 75,000

Cash position is Cr. U.S. $ 75,000. Exchange position is U.S. $ 55,000 (O/B). We may sale spot U.S. $ 55,000 which will bring down cash position to U.S. $ 20,000 and exchange position to square.

Rates

When bank buys foreign exchange from customer, it has to sell the same in the interbank market at the market buying rate. Similarly, while selling foreign exchange to customers, it buys from interbank market at market selling rate.

Everyday in the morning, bank's Treasury Department obtain interbank rates and load appropriate margins before advising the rates to the branches for daily transactions. Rates are broadly the following types:

1. TT Buying
2. Bill Buying
3. TT Selling
4. Bill Selling
5. TC Buying
6. TC Selling
7. Currency Buying
8. Currency Selling

1. **TT Buying:** This is the best buying rate for the customer and is applicable to transactions where foreign exchange is already credited to nostro account. This rate is arrived at from interbank buying rate less exchange margin. Here, exchange margin is the least as bank has already received the funds in its nostro account.

   ABC Bank, Matunga branch has received a money transfer for say, USD 5000 favouring customer 'X'. The message contains "Cover credited to your Account No. with XYZ Bank, NY". This means bank's nostro account XYZ bank has been credited with USD 5000.

2. **Bill Buying:** Transaction where Bank has not received funds but will receive after making a claim to the foreign banks, e.g.,:

   (a) Payment of a foreign currency Demand Draft by an Indian Bank with instruction of the DD issuing bank to "claim cover upon payment".

(b) Discounting of an export bill (here bank has to process papers as well as receive foreign currency payment later). Interbank buying rate less exchange margin more than in TT Buying.

3. **TT Selling:** Clean sale without any paper processing, e.g., Issue of a Demand Draft.

4. **Bill Selling:** Handling of paperwork is involved. Here, exchange margin to be added with interbank selling rate will be higher than in TT Selling.

Example 39: On 31st January, 2013, a forward contract for USD 25000 earlier booked by an importer matured for execution but the customer was unable to honour the contract and requested the bank to extend the sale contract for an additional period of three months. The contract was booked at:

- USD 1 = ₹ 62.00
- USD/INR Quote on 31/1/2013
- Spot 61.45/61.47
- February 1200/1300
- March 2200/2400
- April 3600/3800

What would be the cost to customer for extension of the contract and applicable forward rate for April, 2013?

Margin for TT Buying – 0.1%

Margin for Bill Selling – 0.2%

Solution:

1. This is a case of extension of forward contract.
2. Since the contract was booked by an importer, it is a sale contract.
3. Cancellation of forward sale contract is done at TT Buying Rate.

Hence, we have to cancel the contract at TT Buying Rate.

U.S. Dollar Quote on 31/1/2013

Spot	61.4500 (Buying Rate)
Less: Margin 0.1%	(–) 0.0614
	61.3886

Hence TT Buying Rate would be 61.39

Contracted amount U.S. $ 25000 @ ₹ 61.39	= ₹ 15,34,750
Originally, booked rate U.S. $ 25000 @ ₹ 62.00	= ₹ 15,50,000
Difference against the customer	= ₹ 15,250

Now, a fresh contract needs to be booked for 3 months

Calculation of 3 months forward rate:

Here, since customer is an importer, we have to select spot selling rate first which is:

	61.4700	
Add: April Premium	0.3800	(We need to add as market will take more)
	61.8500	
Add: Margin @ 0.2%	.1237	
	61.9737	

∴ Outright forward rate applicable to customer is U.S. $ = 61.97

6.4 Foreign Exchange Dealers' Association of India

Foreign Exchange Dealers' Association of India (FEDAI) was set up in 1958.

Role of FEDAI

Its major activities include:

- Framing of rules governing the conduct of interbank foreign exchange business *vis-à-vis* public.
- Liaison with RBI for reforms and development of forex market.

Functions

(a) Set guidelines and rules for forex business

(b) Training the bank personnel

(c) Advising/assisting member banks in settling issues/matters in their dealings

(d) Represent members on government/RBI/other bodies

(e) Monitor developments

(f) Identify problems/difficulties

(g) Ensure proper adherence

❋ ❋ ❋

Chapter 7 CAPITAL ADEQUACY NORMS

7.1 The Importance of Capital for a Bank

Like any other business, banks also need capital. But the difference between the bank and any other business like a manufacturing unit or a trading unit is that banks are highly leveraged and have the potential for causing systemic crisis. Banks deal in money and lending money is the principal source of bread and butter. When a loan turns out to be an NPA, bank adopts various tools of recovery but if bank does not succeed in recovery, the amount needs to be written off ultimately from profits. When profits proof to be inadequate, loss has to be made out of capital. As long as capital is sufficient to absorb the loss, banks survive – thereafter collapses. Herein lies the importance of strength of capital.

Capital for a bank can be:

1. Market value of capital
2. Book value of capital
3. Regulatory capital
4. Economic capital

We shall deal with regulatory capital (capital to risk weighted assets).

Internationally, different countries had different capital regulations by respective national regulators. In the 1970s and 1980s, many big banks faced crisis. A German Bank named Bankhaus Herstatt failed in 1974 after which 'Herstatt risk' was named. A serious liquidity crisis was about to take place which was avoided with the help of U.S. Euro dollar banks. Another major crisis took place in 1982 by an Italian Bank named Banko Ambrociano. With these repeated banking crisis taking place, Central bankers from some of the major countries set up Basel Committee of Banking Supervision under the leadership of Bank for International Settlement (BIS) which was entrusted to formulate uniform capital standards on all banks.

7.2 Basel I, II, and III

In 1988, first Basel agreement was signed by G10 countries mainly incorporating relationship between assets and capital. It was stipulated that banks who are party to the accord need to have a capital of 8% of risk-weighted assets in terms of risk profile.

Example 40:

Assets	Amount ₹	Risk Weights %	Resultant Risk-weighted Assets ₹
Cash	10	0	0
Balances with other Bank	10	20	2
Investment in G-Securities	5	0	0
Investment in other securities	5	20	1
Investment in Bonds issued by other Banks	15	20	3
Loan Guaranteed by Govt. of India	5	0	0
Loans to others	50	100	50
Total	100	160	56

Total assets are 100 but risk-weighted assets are 56. So, as per initial Basel Committee Norms **(Basel I)** minimum capital required was 8% of ₹ 56 = ₹ 4.48 against total assets of ₹ 100.

Reserve Bank of India in April 1992 decided to introduce a risk asset ratio system for banks in India including foreign banks as a measure of capital adequacy. Based on the lines of framework of Basel Committee on Banking Supervision (BCBS), initially it took into account only elements of credit risk in different types of assets in the balance sheet as well as off- balance sheet items. Credit Risk, in simple terms, is the risk of loss arising out of default of counterparty. If a loan is given by a bank, the risk that the loan may not be repaid as per terms is credit risk. In 1996, BCBS issued an amendment in the capital accord to incorporate 'Market risk'. Market risk is defined as risk of loss arising out of adverse movement in market value of an asset like stocks, bond, commodity, foreign exchange, derivative contracts, interest rates etc.

Major market risks are liquidity risks, interest rate risks, foreign exchange risks and equity price risks. Reserve Bank of India issued Guideline to Banks on maintenance of capital charge on account of market risks in June 2004. Even though, BIS norms were to maintain capital charge of 8% of Risk-weighted Assets, in India, RBI subsequently instructed all banks to maintain a minimum capital funds of 9% of Risk-weighted Assets. Capital funds consist of Tier-I (paid-up capital, reserves, retained profits etc.) and Tier-II (subordinated debt, hybrid debt instrument, general reserves etc.) Revised Capital Adequacy Framework released by BCBS in June, 2004 was commonly known as **Basel II.**

Basel II adopted a three pillar structure for strengthening of capital:

Pillar 1	Pillar 2	Pillar 3
Minimum Capital Requirement	Supervisory Review	Market Discipline

Minimum Capital Requirement

As explained earlier, banks are required to maintain a capital to Risk-weighted Assets Ratio (CRAR) of 9%. Basel II norms also introduced concept of operational risk. Operational risk was defined by Bank for International Settlements (BIS) as **"the risk of loss resulting from inadequate or failed internal processes, people or systems or from external events".** Basel II further clarified that operational risk includes legal risk but excludes strategic and reputational risk.

A bank should compute its total CRAR requirement as under:

$$\frac{\text{Eligible total capital}}{\text{Credit risk RWA + Market risk RWA + Operational risk RWA}}$$

Example 41:

$$\frac{\text{Eligible total capital ₹7,200}}{\text{Credit risk RWA (₹40,000) + Market risk RWA (₹8,000) + Operational risk RWA (₹12,000)}}$$

CRAR 12%

Similarly, Tier-I CRAR should be computed as:

$$\frac{\text{Eligible Tier I capital}}{\text{Credit risk RWA + Market risk RWA + Operational risk RWA}}$$

7.3 Various Risks Faced by Banks and Calculation of Capital Charge

For calculation of Capital charge on credit risk, three methods were prescribed:

1. Standardized Approach
2. Foundation Capital IRB (Internal Risk Based) Approach
3. Advanced IRB Approach.

Standardized Approach: It uses ratings issued by external rating agencies for calculation of capital requirements. In accounts with limits of ₹ 10 crore and above, services of rating agencies evaluated and approved by Reserve Bank of India only are to be availed of. Risk weights for different assets classes were stipulated in the guideline. For example, risk weights for long-term claims on corporates:

Domestic Rating Agencies	AAA	AA	A	BBB	BB and below	Unrated
Risk Weight (Percentage)	20	30	50	100	150	100

1. Short-term Claims on Corporates:

CARE	CRISIL	Fitch (India Ratings & Research)	ICRA	Brickwork	%
CARE A1+	CRISIL A1 +	Fitch A1+	ICRA A1+	Brickwork A1+	20
CARE A1	CRISIL A1	Fitch A1	ICRA A1	Brickwork A1	30
CARE A2	CRISIL A2	Fitch A2	ICRA A2	Brickwork A2	50
CARE A3	CRISIL A3	Fitch A3	ICRA A3	Brickwork A3	100
CARE A4 and D	CRISIL A4 and D	Fitch A4 and D	ICRA A4 and D	Brickwork A4 and D	150
Unrated	Unrated	Unrated	Unrated	Unrated	100

2. Exposure to Soveriegn:

Central and State Government 0

State Government 20

3. Foreign Soveriegn:

S & P/Fitch rating	AAA to AA	A	BBB	BB to B	Below B	Unrated
Moody's rating	A aa to A a	A	B aa	B a to B	Below B	Unrated
Risk Weights (%)	0	20	50	100	150	100

4. Retail Exposure:

Secured by mortages on residential property:

	Risk Weights %	
	LTV upto 75%	**LTV > 75%**
Upto ₹ 30 lakh	50	100
Above ₹ 30 lakh but below ₹ 75 lakh	75	100
₹ 75 lakh and above	125	125

Restructured housing loans will attract additional risk weights of 25%. Reserve Bank of India may decide to apply 150% or higher risk weight depending on the riskiness of exposure.

Details of risk weights on different exposures like Banks (Indian and Foreign), Public Sector Enterprises, International Organizations can be viewed from RBI Master Circular RBI/2012-13/95 dated July 2, 2012.

Internal Rating Based (IRB) Approach

Under this approach, banks are permitted to use their internal rating system for credit risk. But, this is subject to specific approval of the supervisor. This approach is of two categories.

(a) Foundation IRB approach (FIRB)

(b) Advanced IRB approach (AIRB)

IRB approach allows banks to use their own estimates for credit risk components – Probability of Default (PD), Loss Given Default (LGD), Exposure at Default (EAD) and Effective Maturity (M), in the process of defermination of capital requirement for a specific credit exposure. RBI's approval for banks to adopt IRB approach will be subject to Bank's compliance with all the guidelines and explicit approval. IRB approach basically covers capital calculation for credit risk based upon measures of Expected Losses and Unexpected Losses. For Expected Loss, Banks follow guidelines on provision on corporate, sovereign, Bank and Retail exposures and adjust regulatory capital. For unexpected loss, RBI has specified detail guidelines on risk components and risk-weight functions. Under IRB Guidelines, the following are key factors:

(i) **PD (Probability of Default):** Probability that the borrower will default in a time horizon of one year.

(ii) **LGD (Loss Given Default):** Upon default of a borrower, the loss that the bank will suffer.

(iii) EAD (Exposure at Default): At the time of default, the gross amount that the bank is exposed to.

(iv) M (Effective Maturity): Longest possible residual time, that the borrower is supposed to fulfill the obligation.

1. **Market Risk:** Market risk position for which bank needs to arrive at capital charge include:

   (a) Risk relating to interest rate related securities and equities in the trading book.

   (b) Foreign Exchange Risk.

   Detail guidelines on calculation of market risk has been given in RBI Master Circular No. 13/95 dated July 2, 2012.

   Banks need to manage the market risk on daily basis.

   Minimum capital requirement for securities is expressed in terms of two separately calculated charges:

   (i) Specific Risk

   (ii) General Market Risk

   (i) ***Specific Risk:*** Refers to the risk of adverse movement in the price of an individual security because of reasons concerning individual issuer.

   (ii) ***General Market Risk:*** Refers to interest rate risk in the portfolio and capital requirements for general market risk is supposed to guard against loss arising out of changes in market interest rates.

   Basel Committee specified two broad methods for calculation of capital charge for market risk:

   1. Standardized method

   2. Banks' internal risk management models method.

   Total capital charge for market risk would comprise of:

   (a) Interest Rate (General Market Risk and Specific Risk)

   (b) Equity (General Market Risk and Specific Risk)

   (c) Foreign Exchange and Gold

2. **Operational Risk**: Operational risk is the risk of loss arising out of inadequate or failed internal processes, people and systems or from external events.

   In terms of New Capital Adequacy framework, guidelines of Reserve Bank of India, there are three methods of calculation of capital charges on account of operational risk:

(i) Basic Indicator Approach

(ii) Standardized Approach

(iii) Advanced Measurement Approach

Banks need to develop advanced operational risk measurement systems and practices in order to migrate from one approach to another and onwards.

(i) **Basic Indicator Approach:** Under this approach, banks' capital requirement for operational risk will be equal to 15% of average positive annual gross income over the previous three years. If for any year, the gross income is negative or zero, it should be excluded from calculation. Thus,

Capital charge under –

Basic Indicator Approach:: (∑ (GI i…..n × £)/n

£ = 15 per cent set by BCBS

n = No. of previous three years where gross income is positive

GI = Annual gross income, wherever positive over the previous three years.

Gross Income = Net Profit + Provisions and Contingencies + Operating Expenses.

(ii) **Standardized Approach:** In this approach, banks' business activities are grouped into eight categories. Against each category, capital charge for operational risk is arrived at by multiplying gross income of that business activity with a fixed rate which will be different for different categories.

Business Activity	Fixed Rate
(a) Corporate Finance	18%
(b) Trading	18%
(c) Commercial Banking	15%
(d) Retail Banking	12%
(e) Agency activity	15%
(f) Payment and settlement	18%
(g) Retail Brokerage	12%
(h) Asset Management	12%

(iii) **Advanced Measurement Approach:** Under this approach, banks are permitted to develop their respective statistical models for arriving at necessary capital for operational risk (Internal Management Approach).

Banks need to use statistical tools to arrive at Expected Losses and Unexpected Losses with a maximum confidence level over a period.

Capital charge for each business line and event type = (Rate to be specified by banks subject to supervisory approval, say, 'gama') × (Exposure Indicator for each business line and event type combination) × (Probability of an operational risk event occurring over a time horizon) × (Average Loss if that event does take place) = 'gama' × Expected Loss charged to capital.

Thus, Basel II framework rests on following three pillars:

- Pillar 1 – Minimum capital requirements specifying risk-sensitive calculation of capital requirements for credit, market and operational risk.
- Pillar 2 – Supervisory Review Process (SRP).

This process envisages a particular institution's internal assessment process of capital and its adequacy. It ensures existence of suitable risk management system in banks and their review by the supervisory authority. The following four key principles were laid down in the Basel II document under Pillar 2:

1. Banks to have a process for assessing their level of capital adequacy pursuant to their risk profile as well as a strategy for maintenance of capital levels.
2. It is not enough for banks to have a process for assessment of capital adequacy; supervisors should review and evaluate the assessment and strategies of the banks and also capacity of the banks to monitor and ensure compliance with the required regulatory ratios. In case of unsatisfactory findings, supervisors should take appropriate supervisory action.
3. Banks are expected to hold in excess of minimum regulatory capital ratios and supervisors should require the banks to do so.
4. Supervisors should be prompt to step in from preventing capital from going below the minimum required level in relation to the risk profile of a particular bank and would require quick remedial action, if desired capital is not maintained. Under Supervisory Review Process, banks are required to implement an internal process named **Internal Capital Adequacy Assessment Process (ICAAP)** which is supposed to ensure proper assessment of capital adequacy in proportion to the risk profiles as well as to have a strategy for maintenance of capital levels.

Pillar 2 also stipulates that supervisory activies should subject the banks to an evaluation process called Supervisory Review and Evaluation Process (SREP) and adopt appropriate supervisory measures.

Arising out of above four principles, the following are the responsibilities of banks and supervisors.

1. Banks to have a process for assessment of their overall capital adequacy in relation to the risk profile and also a strategy for maintenance of capital levels.
2. Banks should operate above the required level of minimum regulatory capital ratios.

Responsibilities of Supervisor:

(a) Supervisor should review and monitor banks' ICAAP.

(b) In the event of outcome of the ICAAP being not satisfactory, supervisors need to take appropriate action.

(c) Supervisors need to review and ensure banks' compliance with the regulatory capital ratios.

(d) Supervisor should be able to require banks to hold capital in excess of the minimum holding.

(e) Supervisors need to step in at an early stage so as to prevent capital from falling below minimum levels.

(f) In the event of capital not maintained or restored, supervisors should resort to immediate remedial action.

Thus, two important features of Pillar 2 are ICAAP and Supervisory Review and Evaluation Process (SREP).

ICAAP relates to banks' procedures and measures to comply with the following:

(i) Proper identification and measurement of risks.

(ii) Adequate level of internal capital with regard to the risk profile.

(iii) Development of suitable risk management systems of the bank on an ongoing basis.

SREP deals with review and evaluation process followed by the supervisor which also includes evaluation of banks' ICAAP, conducting an independent assessment of the Bank's risk profile and if need be, taking appropriate action and prudential measures.

- Pillar 3 – Market Discipline – This third pillar seeks to ensure transparency through increasing disclosure requirements by banks. The main objective of this Pillar is to complement the other two pillars, namely minimum capital requirements and supervisory review process by formulating a set of disclosure requirements which will allow market participants to measure the capital adequacy of the institutions.

7.4 Rationale for Basel Agreement

The basic rationale for such a vast and important document applicable internationally are broadly two:

1. **Financial Stability:** Financial stability is considered a public good applicable worldwide. In the event of instability in the world financial system, particularly in the interconnected world that we live in today, everybody suffers. Hence, it is a matter of common interest that there should be a prudent and sound minimum standards.
2. **Avoiding Unhealthy Competition:** Competition of lowering of standards to compete against each other is detrimental to the system. If a bank tries to improve its position at the cost of other and thus compels the other to lower the standard too, a sort of 'beggar thy neighbour' approach will cost the international community. This is another reason that the Basel Committee came to a decision to formulate a set of minimum standards. Basel II, announced in 2004, was much wider in scope and more complex than Basel I particularly with regard to risk coverage and risk management. Basel II, as we have seen, provided for:
   (a) Three-pillar approach
   (b) Capital requirement to take care of operational risk
   (c) Allowed scope for banks which are capable to estimate their capital and using respective models instead of given fixed weights.

But it is also a fact that with all the safeguards of Basel I and Basel II, global financial crisis could not be avoided. Among various reasons that contributed to the crisis, some regulatory and control gaps were clearly observed:

(i) Banking system needed better quality and more quantity of capital.

(ii) Liquidity risk needed more attention.

(iii) Quality of credit analysis needed to be improved.

(iv) Functioning of rating agencies needed to be looked into.

(v) Shadow-banking institutions needed to be brought under strict regulations.

(vi) Formation of asset bubbles needed to be monitored on ongoing basis.

But many of these do not fall within purview of Basel Committee. Post crisis, Basel Committee's recommendation under Basel III comprised mainly on **CAPITAL** and **LIQUIDITY.**

CAPITAL

1. Better quality and more quantity of capital requirement as basic minimum for banks to achieve over a time horizon.
2. Introduction of a capital conservation buffer.
3. Introduction of a 'leverage ratio'.

LIQUIDITY:

1. Liquidity coverage ratio (LCR) which will enable banks to hold liquid assets enough to guard against 30-day stress situation.
2. A net stable funding ratio which will ensure stable sources of funding to take care of long-term assets of the bank.

Basel III Capital Requirements of Banks

(As a Percentage of Risk-weighted Assets)

	Basel III (International)	Basel III (RBI)
Common Equity		
Minimum	4.5	5.5
Capital Conservation Buffer (CCB)	2.5	2.5
Total	7.0	8.0
Tier-I Capital		
Minimum	6.0	7.0
Minimum + CCB	8.5	9.5
Total Capital		
Minimum	8.0	9.0
Minimum + CCB	10.5	11.5

(***Source:*** Reserve Bank of India, Speech of Dr. Duvvuri Subbarao)

1. Tier-I capital ratio increases to 6% from 4%:
   (a) Time allowed is 4.5% from 1/1/2013, 5.5% from 1/1/2014 and 6% from 1/1/2015.
   (b) Common equity requirement of Tier-II increases from 2% to 4.5%.

(c) Time allowed 3.5% from 1/1/2013, 4% from 1/1/2014 and 4.5% from 1/1/2015.

2. Capital Conservation Buffer:

(a) Meant for absorption of losses during periods of economic stress.

(b) Banks are required to build up a capital conservation buffer of 2.5% to sustain periods of stress bringing the total common equity requirement to 7% (RBI direction is 8%).

This capital conservation buffer is to be met only with common equity. Banks unable to maintain capital conservation buffer will have restrictions on dividend payments, share buyback as also bonuses.

Countercyclical Capital Buffer

This is aimed at protection from effects of credit cycle, i.e., when it is felt that credit growth is resulting in an unusual build up of systemic risk.

The buffer will vary between 0-2.5% of common equity or other fully loss absorbing capital depending on the views and judgment of respective jurisdictions while taking a view of the extent of systemic risk built up in a given territory.

1. **Liquidity Standard:** To ensure the system to be insulated against liquidity risk, the following measures are specified.

2. **Liquidity Coverage Ratio (LCR):** Banks need to have sufficient unencumbered high quality liquid assets to survive a 30-day stress scenario. LCR is primarily intended to safeguard banks' short-term liquidity needs.

The time horizon for introduction of LCR commencing from January 1, 2015 till January 2019.

Minimum LCR requirements:

2015	2016	2017	2018	2019
60%	70%	80%	90%	100%

LCR will have two components:

(i) Value of the stock of high quality liquid assets (HQLA).

(ii) Total net cash flows expressed as:

$$\text{LCR} = \frac{\text{Stock of HQLA}}{\text{Total net cash outflows over the next 30 calender days}} \geq 100\%$$

***

Net Stable Funding Ratio (NSFR)

NSFR is a long-term ratio which measures the amount of stable funding a firm has to continue to survive a year-long liquidity crisis.

$$\text{NSFR} = \frac{\text{Available amount of stable funding}}{\text{Required amount of stable funding}} \geq 0$$

The objective of NSFR is to ensure more medium-and long-term funding of assets and activities of banking organizations.

The new LCR and NSFR will entail costs as well as benefits. Rules under Basel III will change behavior of banks. Banks will bring down risky liquidity holdings. Competition for garnering share of low-cost funds will increase. A quantitative study by the Basel Committee on Banking Supervision shows that Banks worldwide need additional capital of Euro 175 billion to reach a core capital ratio of 4.5% and around 600 billion for 7% requirement (Speech by President of Netherland Bank and Chairman of BCBS during ING Basel III Financing Conference, April 14, 2011).

In terms of the Basel Committee estimate, if bank capital goes up by 2%, the risk of a crisis goes down by 50%. Thus, there would be a significant increase in a market confidence upon successful implementation of Basel III and the shock-absorbing capacity of Banking sector will be much higher.

For controlling leverage, 3% non-risk based leverage ratio including off-balance sheet exposures will act as a backstop to the risk-based capital requirement mentioned above. This would contain build up of leverage on the system.

Basel III, unlike Basel I and II is equipped to address risks at both the individual level as well as systemic level (known as micro-prudential and macro-prudential approach).

At the individual level, there will be:

(a) Higher risk coverage supported by leverage ratio.

(b) Stringent definition of capital with higher emphasis on common equity.

(c) Improvement in Supervisory Review Process and market discipline (Pillar 2 and 3).

At the systemic level, there will be:

(a) Introduction of capital buffer in good times to be utilized in bad times.

(b) Leverage Ratio will also benefit the system levels.

❋ ❋ ❋

SOME QUESTIONS

1. For the purpose of financial inclusion, banks are opening "BSBDA" Accounts. What are the features of "BSBDA – SMALL" Account?

Ans. (a) Adult individuals can open such accounts upon giving a declaration that credit balance will not exceed ₹ 50,000 and total credits in a year will not exceed ₹ 1 lakh.

(b) Firms/Joint accounts are not eligible.

(c) Simplified Know Your Customer norms to be complied with.

(d) Account can be opened with zero balance and no minimum balance criteria is applicable.

(e) Total of debits cannot exceed ₹ 10,000 in a month.

(f) Foreign remittances cannot be credited without completing normal KYC requirements.

(g) Small Accounts are valid for 12 months extendable by another 12 months provided the person can satisfy having applied for an officially valid document.

Account can be converted into normal SB Account by maintaining required minimum balance. All the existing "No-frills accounts" are to be treated as "BSBDA" accounts w.e.f. 10.8.2012

2. What are the broad features and advantages of Recurring Deposits?

Ans. Broad Features:

- Recurring Deposit account can be opened for a minimum period of 12 months and a maximum period of 120 months.
- The amount of installment once fixed, cannot be changed.
- Installment is to be paid on or before the last working day of the month.

Advantage:

- Interest earned under this scheme is not subject to TDS.

3. What are the characteristics of Retail Loan?

Ans.
- These are small ticket loans (There is no hard and fast definition for small).
- These loans meet the needs of a large number of customers with well diversified portfolios.
- The customers are generally individuals or small organizations.
- These loans offer standard ready-to-use products to customers. Very rarely, a customer's requirement is customized.
- Credit decisions for such loans are quick and more streamlined.
- High number of transactions and high volume.
- Transactions being high, supervision and monitoring costs are also high.
- Interest yield is relatively higher.

4. What is KYC?

Ans. Know Your Customer (KYC) primarily involves:

(i) Identification of the customer

(ii) Address proof – approved documents like PAN Card, Passport, Utility Bills, etc. should be produced to the bank along with self attested Xerox copies for compliance.

KYC is applicable to every individual who wants to have any business relationship with the bank. This means, any individual wanting to open an account (savings or current account and recurring or fixed deposit), open a locker, receive any benefits on account of financial transactions, remittance or wire transfer, and apply for a loan is subject to KYC.

The KYC norm has been validated under Section 35A of the Banking Regulation Act, 1949, and Rule 7 of the Prevention of Money Laundering Rules, 2005. Any violation of these norms could attract severe penalty under the BR Act.

CASE STUDY

Situation A:

A well dressed person, excellent in communication approaches you as a Branch Manager posted in a tier-II town and introduces himself as a Businessman having business interest in various East African countries dealing in metal scraps. During conversation with you, he states that he has decided to set up a Branch office business at your center. The person wants to open a current account in his personal name so as to facilitate transfer of funds. In the midst of conversation, he makes a call to somebody to transfer USD 250000, in equivalent Indian Rupees to his account to be opened at your branch and that he would inform the account number in an hours' time. He seemed extremely busy and hurrying up for completion of formalities. In the meanwhile, he makes another call apparently to his travel agent enquiring of his visa formalities for Indonesia and South Korea.

When you insist on his proof of identity, he shows you copy of passport saying that original is with travel agent for visa purpose. As he is supposed to travel out of the country next day onwards for a week or so, he promises to show you the original passport during his next visit after 10-12 days. He has also taken an office space on rent at your centre and shows the agreement and requests you to take the agreement as a proof of address. But he desires opening of the account immediately as some payments are to be made in about 2-3 days.

Your branch is lagging behind deposit target by about ₹ 75 lakh and this one account itself is likely to exceed your target.

How would you respond to the customer?

Answer to Case Study (Situation A)

Do not open the account without original identity and address proof to bank's satisfaction. Politely explain to the customer about the regulations. At the most, you can tell him that as a special case the account can be opened but no transactions will be allowed till submission of the required documents.

Do Banks open accounts for those without an address proof?

Yes. But such individuals have to submit an identity document along with a utility bill of the relative with whom the prospective customer is living and a declaration from the relative that the said person is a relative.

Can KYC Norms be relaxed?

To ensure financial inclusion, a low-income group customer without identity and address proofs can open a bank account with an introduction from another account holder who has fulfilled the bank's KYC procedure. The introducer's account with the bank should be at least six months old and should show satisfactory transactions.

Can banks ask customers to re-submit fresh KYC document?

Banks can ask customers to re-submit fresh identification and address proof to update their records. They can also ask for additional documents if they have doubts about some transaction in order to prevent the account from being used for money laundering, terrorist or criminal activities.

5. Following is the position of a C/C account:

Sanctioned Limit		–	₹ 1,60,000	
Drawing Limit		–	₹ 80,000	
		Dr.	Cr.	Bal
21/1/2013	Balance b/f		___	Dr. ₹ 55,000
27/3/2013	Interest	1500		Dr. ₹ 56,500

Will the account be a standard asset or NPA as on 31/3/2013? Give reasons.

Ans. Since there is no credit for 3 months, the account will be NPA as on 31/3/2013.

6. In a loan account (NPA – Category Doubtful for 2 years), Balance outstanding is Dr. ₹ 1.25 lakh. Security: Hypothecation of stock of paints and chemicals and personal guarantee of wife of partners. Your visit to the unit shows hardly any stock. In answer to your recall notice addressed to borrower/guarantors, the borrower offers you a compromise settlement with ₹ 30,000. How would you deal with the situation?

Ans. There cannot be any one definitive answer. But prudence suggests that security being negligible, legal action or seizure will not yield any benefit. Since, partners' wives guarantees are there, efforts should be made to increase the compromise amount through repeated meetings including threatening suits against the borrower/guarantors and settle the dues by stretching the offer to the maximum, arriving at a compromise settlement and writing off the balance.

7. What is an 'Out of Order' Status?

Ans. An account is termed 'Out of Order' if the balance outstanding in the account is in excess of sanctioned limit or drawing limit. Other reasons also include non-renewal of account in time,non-submission of stock statements etc.

8. What are the different classes of Non-performing Assets (NPAs)?

Ans. (i) Substandard Assets

(ii) Doubtful Assets

(iii) Loss Assets

9. Explain the 'Internal' and 'External' reasons for a borrowal account becoming Non-performing?

Ans. Internal:

(a) Willful default

(b) Managerial incompetence

(c) Financial indiscipline

(d) Internal dispute among partners/co-promoters/unhealthy labour relations

(e) Technological obsolescence

(f) Faulty Machinery causing substandard products

(g) Inventory pile up

(h) Delay in receivable collection

(i) High Staff Turnover

(j) Diversion/Siphoning of funds

External:

(a) Economic slow down and depressed market

(b) Changes in Government policies

(c) Strikes and riots

(d) Poor loan repayment environments due to wrong publicity by vested interest group

(e) Shortage of inputs

(f) Infrastructural deficiency

10. What are the broad tools of NPA Management?

Ans. (a) Vigorous follow-up

(b) Recovery Camps

(c) Lok Adalat

(d) SARFAESI Act

(e) Debt Recovery Tribunals

(f) Compromise

11. Explain the main features of credit policy.

Ans. (a) Improvement and maintenance of asset quality

(b) Focus on priority sector lending including Agriculture, SME and Export Credit

(c) Financial Inclusion

(d) Improvement of risk-adjusted return and increasing market share

12. What are the 'fund-based' and 'non-fund based' exposures?

Ans. *(i)* ***Fund-based Exposures:*** Any lending activity where outlay of fund is involved, i.e., borrower receives funds. Example: Cash credit, overdraft, Term loan, Bill finance etc.

(ii) ***Non-fund Based Exposures:*** Any lending facility where borrower does not receive funds but receives the benefit on the strength of bank's reputation. Example: Letter of Credit, Guarantees, Acceptances, exposure in financial derivatives etc.

13. What is the purpose of Term Loan?

Ans. Financing of fixed assets, e.g., acquiring land and building, factory including Plant and Machinery, constructing shed etc.

14. What is the purpose of Cash Credit?

Ans. Financing of stock of raw materials, work-in-process, semi-finished goods, etc.

15. What is Financial Inclusion?

Ans. Financial Inclusion is "the process of ensuing access to appropriate financial products and services needed by all sections of the society in general and vulnerable groups such as weaker sections and low-income groups, in particular at an affordable cost, in a fair and transparent manner by regulated, mainstream institutional players". (Source: Reserve Bank of India)

16. What is Business Facilitator? Explain its services.

Ans. Business Facilitator (BF) ideally is from the village or the area he is supposed to serve and should have knowledge about the livelihood pattern, profile of the farmers and others in the village. Facilitation services are mainly the following including credit counseling:

(i) Identification of borrowers

(ii) Creating awareness about savings, education and advice on managing money and debt counseling and other products

(iii) Collection, processing and submission of loan applications to banks

(iv) Preliminary verification of information

(v) Nurturing SHGs/Joint Liability Groups (JLGs)

(vi) Post-sanction monitoring

(vii) Follow-up for recovery

17. Explain the major functions of Business Correspondents.

Ans. (a) Mobilization of small deposits

(b) Disbursement of small loans

(c) Recovery and collection of principal and interest

(d) Sale of third party products

(e) Handling remittances of small value

18. Explain the eligibility norms for selection of BCs.

Ans. (a) NGOs/MFIs/Societies/Companies incorporated u/s 25 of Companies Act, 1956.

(b) Registered NBFC not engaged in accepting Public Deposits. Objective clause of the registered entities should specifically contain authority to act as BC.

(c) Good track record of the office bearers. Institutions or its office-bearers must not be a defaulter to any bank/financial institution.

(d) Retired bank/government employees/ex-servicemen.

19. What are the different categories of Priority Sector Lending?

Ans. (i) Agriculture (Direct and Indirect)

(ii) Micro and Small Enterprises

(iii) Service Enterprises

(iv) Micro Credit

20. Who are eligible to be covered under weaker section?

Ans. (a) Small and marginal farmers with land holding of 5 acres and less, and landless labourers, tenant farmers and share-croppers.

(b) Artisans, village and cottage industries where individual credit limits do not exceed ₹ 50,000.

(c) Beneficiaries for Swarnajayanti Gram Swarozgar Yojna (SGSY) now National Rural Livelihood Mission (NRLM).

(d) Scheduled Castes and Scheduled Tribes.

(e) Beneficiaries of Differential Rate of Interest (DRI) Scheme.

(f) Beneficiaries under Swarna Jayanti Sahari Rozgar Yojana (SJSRY).

(g) Beneficiaries under the Scheme for Rehabilitation of Manual Scavengers (SRMS).

(h) Advances to Self Help Groups (SHGs).

(i) Loans to distressed poor to prepay their debt to informal sector, against appropriate collateral or group security.

(j) Loans granted under (1) to (9) above to persons from minority communities as may be notified by Government of India from time to time.

21. What are the limits of Housing Loans under Priority Sector?

Ans. Loans upto ₹ 25 lakh for construction or purchase of residential units per family (excluding loans sanctioned by Banks to their own employees) as well as loans for repairs upto ₹ 1 lakh in rural areas and ₹ 2 lakh in urban and metropolitan areas are eligible for classification under priority sector.

22. What is the Permissible Disposal Time for Applications under Priority Sector?

Ans.

Amount Applied for	Disposal Time
Upto credit limit of ₹ 25,000	Fortnight
Over ₹ 25,000	8-9 weeks
Micro and Small Enterprises upto a limit of ₹ 25,000	2 weeks
Micro and Small Enterprises upto a limit of ₹ 5 lakh	4 weeks

23. Can applications from SC/ST applicants under priority sector be rejected by the sanctioning authority?

Ans. No. Rejections in such cases should be done by an authority higher than the sanctioning authority.

24. Which are the 5 Cs of credit generally insisted upon by bankers?

Ans. (a) Character

(b) Capital

(c) Capacity

(d) Conditions

(e) Collateral

25. In case of corporate borrowers, if the proponent is enjoying banking facilities with other banks, what needs to be done?

Ans. (i) A status report is to be obtained from the banker apart from credit score reports from CIBIL.

(ii) Credit officer must visit the Bank personally and talk to his counterpart of the other Bank to elicit the details of the conduct of the account.

(iii) The findings should be recorded on the credit file.

(iv) If the proponent is also an exporter, RBI/Export Credit Guarantee Corporation list of defaulters should be checked.

26. What is Channel Credit?

Ans. Under this scheme, suppliers to corporates/manufacturing units/distributors are extended financial assistance.

27. What is a Commercial Paper (CP)?

Ans. A Money Market instrument meant for well rated corporates for raising short-term borrowings from the market. It is an unsecured promissory note issued for minimum 7 days and maximum 1 year.

28. Explain the risks in International Trade.

Ans. *(a)* ***Country Risks:*** Political Stability, Economic Environment, Legal system, Forex transactions

(b) ***Forex Risks***

(c) ***Commercial Risks:*** Dependability, Trade disputes

29. What is a Documentary Credit?

Ans. A written undertaking by the Importer's Bank on behalf of its customer, promising to effect payment to exporter upto a stated sum of money within a prescribed time limit and against stipulated documents.

30. Why is an LC beneficial for exporter?

Ans. Exporter is assured of payment upon submission of only stipulated documents in terms of the LC irrespective of risk arising out of unknown buyer, dispute concerning consignment etc.

31. What is UCPDC?

Ans. Uniforms Customs and Practices for Documentary Credits (UCPDC). These are body of rules published by International Chamber of Commerce (ICC) for operation of Letter of Credit mechanism. These rules are revised by ICC from time to time which were first published in 1933 and have undergone six revisions thereafter. Present set of rules is known as UCPDC 600 because they were published in ICC Brochure No. 600 and are in force since 1st July, 2007.

32. How does forfaiting differ from factoring?

Ans.

Factoring	Forfaiting
Usually with recourse	Only without recourse
Continuing transactions	One-time transaction
Mostly consumer goods	Usually capital goods, large projects

33. Explain the important functions of Integrated Treasury.

Ans. (a) Management of Funds

(b) Pricing of Products

(c) Maintenance of statutory requirements

(d) Cash Reserve Ratio

(e) Statutory Liquidity Ratio

(g) Foreign Exchange operations

(h) Investments – maximization of returns

(i) Asset-Liability Management

(j) Controlling market risk

(k) Compliance of Regulatory Requirement

(l) Nostro Reconciliation

34. What is Asset-Liability Management (ALM)? Explain the challenges faced by banks.

Ans. ALM in India has gained importance as a result of changing scenario of Indian Banking System. It was not important when interest rates were fixed and governed by Central Bank of the country and Banks functioned in a regulated market with assured interest margins. There was no threat to survival. Gradually, Banks have started functioning with increasing freedom, facing integration of domestic and global markets with a feeling of threat to survival. Banks mainly faced the following challenges:

(a) Risk Management

(b) Return on Capital

(c) Balance between Risk and Return

35. Explain the aims and objectives of ALM.

Ans. An objective of ALM is not to eliminate risk but to manage. Institutions need to take risk but must know what it is doing. Broadly, the objective of ALM is to control the volatility of Net Interest Income (NII), liquidity risk and ensure a balance between profitability and growth.

Thus, ALM mainly attempts to control market risk which is a function of:

(a) Liquidity Risk

(b) Interest Rate Risk

(c) Currency Risk

ALM also aims at Balance Sheet Management.

36. What is Duration?

Ans. Duration is a measure of price volatility. It is the weighted average maturity of assets/liabilities/off-balance sheet items where present values of all cash flows are used as weights. In effect, Duration is a measure of actual maturity that takes into account timing and size of a security's cash flows.

37. What is the function of Front Office?

Ans. *(i)* ***Dealing – Foreign Exchange, Merchant and Interbank:*** Here, dealers buy, sells, borrow or lend currencies/securities through screen-based trading. Depending on the size and volume of business of a bank, it will have number of dealers, both in money market and foreign exchange market. One bank may have one dealer in one currency or one dealer for various currencies or more than one dealer for one currency.

(ii) ***Money Market:*** Funds Management, Cash Reserve Ratio

(iii) ***Fixed Income:*** SLR (Statutory Liquidity Ratio) and Non-SLR Management

(iv) ***Equity:*** IPOs and Secondary market

(v) ***Derivatives:*** Trading for customers

38. In ALM, what are the prescribed prudential norms for negative mismatches in a structural gap statement as a percentage of outflows?

Ans.

Time Bucket	Negative GAPs as % of outflows
1 day	Not to exceed 5%
2-7 days	Not to exceed 10%
8-14 days	Not to exceed 15%
15-28 days	Not to exceed 20%
Rest time buckets	Individual banks to prescribed

39. Balance Sheet for Excellent Bank.

(Amount in ₹ lakh)

	Assets	Yield		Liabilities	Cost
Rate Sensitive Fixed Rate	1000 700	8% 11%	Rate Sensitive Fixed Rate	1200 440	4% 6%
Non-earning	300		Non-earning	200	
			Equity	160	
	2000			2000	

Find out: (1) NII (2) NIM (3) GAP

Ans. NII = 0.08 (1000) + 0.11 (₹ 700) – 0.04 (₹ 1200) – 0.06 (440)

= (80 + 77) – (48 + 26.4)

= 157 – 74.4

= 82.6

NIM = 82.6/1700

= 4.86%

Gap = ₹ 1000 – ₹ 1200

= ₹ – 200

40. What is the minimum requirement of capital funds for Indian Banks?

Ans: Banks need to maintain a minium capital to Risk-weighted Assets ratio of 9 per cent on an on going basis.

❋ ❋ ❋

ANNEXURE I

Check List of Some Documents Required from Borrowers

1. Application in prescribed format, CMA data form etc. as may be applicable.
2. Details of promoter/s and guarantor/s.
3. Statement of Assets and Liabilities certified by a Chartered Accountant or copies of Income Tax/Wealth Tax Returns for past 3 years.
4. Copies of Memorandum of Association and Articles of Association (for limited companies).
5. Audited Balance Sheets and Profit and Loss Account of the applicant company for past 3 years.
6. Projected Profit and Loss Account and Balance Sheets for next 5 years.
7. Details of Technical Personnel.
8. List of shareholders.
9. Note on Company's tax payment status.
10. Details of Fixed Assets.
11. Particulars of credit facilities including Foreign Currency Loans/other banking facilities enjoyed by the applicant from other banks/financial institutions.
12. Project techno-economic Feasibility Report.
13. Copies of clearances from Government/Local Bodies as may be required in this particular case.
14. Copy of Sale/Lease Deed for land.
15. Copy of document evidencing the land as industrial land.
16. Details of plant and machinery.
17. Evidence of availability of adequate power and water.
18. Arrangement for effluent disposal and waste management.
19. If any bank/financial institution has agreed to extend term loan or working capital loan, copies of such letters.

ANNEXURE II

Check List of Information Required for

(a) Working Capital facilities of lower amounts (usually less than ₹ 10 lakh) .

1. Audited/Unaudited Profit and Loss Account and Balance Sheet for last 3 years.
2. Copies of Assessment Orders/Sales Tax Returns, if available.
3. Current years projections of sales, gross profit and net profit for current year.

(b) Working Capital facilities of higher amounts of ₹ 10 lakh and above.

1. Audited Profit and Loss Account and Balance Sheets.
2. Full set of CMA data forms.
3. Cash flow statement.

ANNEXURE III

Some Common Facilities Granted by Bank

Sr. No.	Purpose of Finance	Facilities (Fund Based)	Principal Security
1	For purchase of land and construction of shed/factory	Term Loan	Equitable mortgage by deposit of title deeds or legal mortgage if equitable mortgage is not possible.
2	For purchase of movable machinery, transport vehicles for own use for transporting raw products, equipment etc.	LC (particularly in the case of Imports) Term Loan/Demand Loan	Depends on terms of sanction; usually cash margin or pledge of TDRs. Hypothecation of movable machinery or road transport vehicles as the case may be.
3	For purchase and holding stocks of raw materials/work-in-process/finished goods/spares	Cash Credit/Bill purchase	Pledge/hypothecation of stocks
4	Financing receivables	Cash Credit Documentary Bills Purchase (D/P) Documentary Bills Discount (B/D) Documentary Bills Purchase (D/A) Supply Bills Purchase	Hypothecation of Book Debts Pledge of transport documents etc.
5	Pre-shipment credit	Packing Credit	Export Trust Receipt Hypothecation of Stocks letter of credit

ANNEXURE IV(i)

Draft

USD 400,000__________ Mumbai March 15, 2013

At Sight____

Pay to the order of M/s. KB Pvt. Ltd. ______________________

Four hundred thousand U.S. Dollars ______________________

for Value Received and charge same to the Account of__________________

To:

New Bank of Singapore,
Robin Road,
Singapore.

Signature_____________
M/s KB Pvt. Ltd.

ANNEXURE IV(ii)

INVOICE

M/s KB Pvt. Ltd.
Ashok Nagar,
Kandivli (East),
Mumbai 400 101.
Mob: 09833393830
Tel: (022) 28852283
March 10, 2013

Sold to: M/s Manosij Bhattacharyya

Terms: Documentary Credit

Invoice No. 741

Contract No. 1713

Packaging	Description	Price (USD)
1 Container	100% cotton shirts as follows:	
	5500 pieces (size 40)	104,500
	7000 pieces (size 42)	143, 500
	Trousers	
	3800 pieces (size 36)	136,800
	Freight	14,000
	Handling	1,200
	CFR, Singapore	400,000

Signature ____________________

Krishna Bhattacharyya

ANNEXURE IV(iii)

<table>
<tr><td rowspan="2">Consignor:
Krishna Bhattacharyya
Ashok Nagar, Kandivli (E),
Mumbai 400 101.</td><td>No.12345</td><td>Original</td></tr>
<tr><td colspan="2">Certificate of Origin</td></tr>
<tr><td>Consignee:
New Bank of India
Robin Road,
Singapore.</td><td>Country of Origin:
INDIA</td><td></td></tr>
<tr><td>Transport Details:
Ocean
MV Puplu</td><td colspan="2"></td></tr>
<tr><td colspan="3">Item, number, marks, number and type of packages, description of goods:
Container:
Containing Shirts and Trousers as per Purchase Order No. 1713</td></tr>
<tr><td colspan="3"></td></tr>
<tr><td colspan="3">The undersigned authority certifies that the goods described above originate in the country shown above.
FEDERATION OF INDIAN CHAMBER OF COMMERCE
Place and date of issue, name and signature of competent authority

March 10, 2013

Signature ______________________
Federation of Indian Chamber of Commerce</td></tr>
</table>

ANNEXURE IV(iv)

<table>
<tr><td colspan="2" rowspan="2">Shipper:
M/s KB Pvt. Ltd.</td><td>Voyage No. 22B</td><td>??? No. 2</td></tr>
<tr><td colspan="2">Shipper's Reference: BBB-22-2424</td></tr>
<tr><td colspan="2">Consignee:
M/s. New Bank of Singapore,
Singapore.</td><td colspan="2">Carrier:
VSK Lines</td></tr>
<tr><td colspan="2">Notify address (carrier not responsible for failure to notify)
Mr. Jeffrey Chow
142, Orioll Crescent,
Singapore.</td><td colspan="2">Place of receipt (Applicable only when document used for MULTIMODAL Transport)</td></tr>
<tr><td>Green Vessel:
M/V Altamares</td><td>Port of Loading:
Hong Kong</td><td colspan="2" rowspan="2">Place of delivery (Applicable only when document used for MULTIMODEL Transport)</td></tr>
<tr><td>Port of Discharge:
Puerto Armuelies
Panama</td><td></td></tr>
<tr><td colspan="4">Container Nos. Seal Nos. Marks and Nos. Number and type of packages description of goods Gross Wt (Kg) Measurements (Cbm)

1 Container 100% Cotton shirts of Indian origin

ON BOARD
March 10, 2013

ABOVE PARTICULARS AS DECLARED BY SHIPPERS</td></tr>
<tr><td colspan="2">Total No. of Containers/Packages Received by the Carriers</td><td>Shippers declared value
USD 400,000</td><td>RECEIVED from the Shipper in apparent good order and condition (unless otherwise noted herein) the total number or quantity of containers or other packa-ges or units indicated in the box opposite entitled total number of containers/packa - ges received by the carrier for carriage subject to all the terms and conditions hereof (including the terms and conditions on the reverse and the terms and conditions of the carriers applicable tariff from the Place of Receipt or the Port of Loading, whichever is applicable) to</td></tr>
</table>

				the Port of Discharge or the Place of Delivery, whichever is applicable. In accepting this document, the Merchant expressly accepts and agrees to all its terms and conditions whether printed stamped or written or otherwise incorporated not withstanding the non signing of this document by the Merchant.
Movement			Freight payable at:	Place and Date of Issue: March 10, 2013, Mumbai
Freight and Charge		Collect	Number of Originals issued 1.	Signature (Company as Agent)
Freight and Charge				
Origin THC/LCL charge				
Sea Freight				
Sea Freight				
Destination Land Freight/Transp Add'l				
Collect USD		14,000		
Appropriate columns to be marked by 'X'				

ANNEXURE V

<table>
<tr><td>Name of Issuing Bank:
New Bank of Singapore
Robin Road,
Singapore.</td><td>Irrevocable Documentary
Credit
No.23456</td></tr>
<tr><td>Place and Date of Issue: Singapore, January 15, 2013</td><td>Beneficiary:
M/s. KB Pvt. Ltd., Flat No. 1703, Bhoomi Arkade, Ashok Nagar, Kandivli (E), Mumbai 400101.</td></tr>
<tr><td>Applicant:
M/s. MB Pvt. Ltd.
Flat No.1406, Katong Park Tower, Singapore.</td><td>Expiry date and place for
Presentation of documents: March 14th, 2013, Mumbai, India.</td></tr>
<tr><td>Advising Bank :
Excellent Bank
Mumbai, India.</td><td>Amount : USD 350,000</td></tr>
<tr><td>Partial Shipment: Not allowed
Transhipment: Not allowed</td><td>Credit available with nominated Bank: By negotiation with Wonderful Bank, Mumbai</td></tr>
<tr><td>Shipment from Port of Mumbai for transportation to Singapore not later than March 7th, 2013</td><td></td></tr>
<tr><td colspan="2">Signed Commercial Invoice
Certificate of Origin
Full set of clean "on board" ocean bills of lading, consigned to order New Bank of Singapore, Singapore.
Covering: 100% cotton shirts of Indian origin size 40 (5500 pieces), size 42 (7000 pieces), size 44 (6000 pieces), trousers (4000 pieces) in terms of Purchase Order No. 1703 CFR Singapore, Incoterms 2000.
Draft to be marked "Drawn under New Bank of Singapore, Documentary Credit No. 23456 issued on January 15th, 2013".</td></tr>
<tr><td colspan="2">Documents to be presented within 21 days from the date of shipment but within the validity of the credit.</td></tr>
<tr><td colspan="2">Usual undertaking as per UCPDC.

____
Name and Signature of the Issuing Bank</td></tr>
</table>

ANNEXURE V(a)

Specimen Letter of Credit Transmitted through SWIFT

SWIFT Letter of Credit in favour of M/s KB Pvt. Ltd., Mumbai Issued by New Bank of Singapore, Singapore.

FIN MESSAGE: (1: F01SWFBOIKC2345)

700 Issue of a Documentary Credit

- **20:** Documentary credit number:
  23456
- **31C:** Date of Issue:
  January 15, 2013
- **31D:** Date and Place of expiry:
  March 14, 2013, Mumbai
- **50:** Applicant:
  M/s MB Pvt. Ltd., Singapore
  Flat No. 1406, Katong Park Tower, Singapore.
- **59:** Beneficiary:
  M/s KB & Pvt. Ltd.
  Flat No. 1703, Bhoomi Arkade,
  Ashok Nagar, Kandivli (E),
  Mumbai 400101.
  32B/Currency Code, Amount
  Currency Code: U.S. Dollar
  Amount: 350,000
- **41D:** Available with:
  Any bank in Mumbai
  By: Negotiation
- **42C:** Drafts at:
  Sight for full invoice value
- **43T:** Transhipment:
  Not permitted
- **44A:** On board/dispatch/taking charge:
  Mumbai
- **44B:** For transportation to:
  Singapore
- **44C:** Latest date of shipment:
  March 7, 2013

- **45A:** Description of goods and/or services:

  100% cotton shirts of Indian origin size 40 (5500 pieces), size 42 (7000 pieces), size 44 (6000 pieces), trousers (4000 pieces) in terms of purchase order no 1703,

  CFR: Singapore, Incoterms 2000
- **46A:** Documents required:
  (a) + Signed commercial invoices showing description of goods in detail.
  (b) + Insurance certificate covering all risks as per institute cargo clause a claims payable at Singapore
  (c) + Certificate of quality issued by SGS
  (d) + Certificate of origin issued by Chamber of Commerce
  (e) + Full set of 3/3 clean on board marine bill of lading consigned to order New Bank of Singapore, Singapore marked freight paid.
- **47A:** Additional conditions:
  (a) Draft to be marked "Drawn under New Bank of Singapore". Documentary Credit No. 23456 issued on January 15, 2013.
  (b) Transport documents must not be dated prior to the date of the credit.
- **48:** Period for Presentation:

  Within 21 days of issue of the transport documents but within the validity of the credit.
- **49:** Confirmation condition:

  Confirmed
- **78:** Instructions to pay/accept/negotiate bank:

  Upon receipt of the credit confirming documents at the counters of issuing bank, payment shall be made for the value of negotiation.
- **72:** Sender to receiver information: This credit is subject to the Uniform Customs and practice for Documentary Credits ICC Publication No. 600.
- **57A**: Advice through Bank: BIC VBSSDEF0222 (Outstanding Bank)
- **MAC:** Authentication Code:

  20B40BAA
- **TRN:** Transaction Reference No.

  0204/BB/29/38

ANNEXURE VI

Section 1

1. Agriculture Direct Finance

1.1 Finance to individual farmers [including Self Help Groups (SHGs) or Joint Liability Groups, (JLGs), i.e., groups of individual farmers, provided banks maintain disaggregated data on such finance for Agriculture and Allied Activities (dairy, fishery, piggery, poultry bee-keeping etc.)

(a) Short-term loans for raising crops, i.e., for crop loans. This will include traditional non-traditional plantations and horticulture.

(b) Advance of ₹ 10 lakh against pledge/hypothecation of agricultural produce (including warehouse receipts) for a period not exceeding 12 months, irrespective of whether the farmers were given crop loans for raising the produce or not.

(c) Working capital and term loans for financing production and investment requirements for agriculture and allied activities.

(d) Loans to small and marginal farmers for purchase of land for agricultural purposes.

(e) Loans to distressed farmers indebted to non-institutional lenders, against appropriate collateral or group security.

(f) Loans granted for pre-harvest and post-harvest activities such as spraying, weeding, harvesting, grading, sorting, processing and transporting undertaken by individuals, SHGs and cooperatives in rural areas.

(g) Loans granted for agricultural and allied activities, irrespective of whether the borrowing entity is engaged in export or otherwise. The export credit granted by RRBs for agricultural and allied activities may, however, be reported separately under heading "Export Credit to Agricultural Sector".

1.2 Finance to others [such as corporates, partnership firms and institutions] for agriculture and allied activities (dairy, fishery, piggery, poultry, bee-keeping, etc.).

(a) Loans granted for pre-harvest and post-harvest activities such as spraying, weeding, harvesting, grading, sorting and transporting.

(b) Finance up to an aggregate amount of ₹ one crore per borrower for the purposes listed at [1.1(a), (b), (c)] and [1.2 (a)] above.

(c) One-third of loans in excess of ₹ one crore in aggregate per borrower for agriculture and allied activities.

Indirect Finance

1.3 Finance for Agriculture and Allied Activities

(a) Two-third of loans to entities covered under 1.2 above in excess of ₹ one crore in aggregate per borrower for agriculture and allied activities.

(b) Loans to food and agro-based processing units with investments in plant and machinery up to 10 crore, undertaken by those other than [1.1(f)] above. Credit under the dairy segment which may primarily benefit small/marginal farmers and tiny units and may contribute to the development of dairy business.

(c) (i) Credit for purchase and distribution of fertilizers, pesticides, seeds, etc.

(ii) Loans up to ₹ 40 lakh granted for purchase and distribution of inputs for the allied activities such as cattle feed, poultry feed, etc.

(d) Finance for setting up of Agriclinics and Agribusiness Centres.

(e) Finance for hire-purchase schemes for distribution of agricultural machinery and implements.

(f) Loans to farmers through Primary Agricultural Credit Societies (PACS), Farmers' Service Societies (FSS) and Large-sized Adivasi Multi Purpose Societies (LAMPS).

(g) Loans to cooperative societies of farmers for disposing of the produce of members.

(h) Financing the farmers indirectly through the cooperative system (otherwise than by subscription to bonds and debenture issues).

(i) Loans for construction and running of storage facilities (warehouse, market yards, godowns, and silos), including cold storage units designed to store agriculture produce/products, irrespective of their location. If the storage unit is registered as SSI unit/micro or small enterprise, the loans granted to such units may be classified under advances to Small Enterprises sector.

(j) Advances to Custom Service Units managed by individuals, institutions or organizations who maintain a fleet of tractors, bulldozers, well-boring equipment, threshers, combines, etc., and undertake work for farmers on contract basis.

(k) Finance extended to dealers in drip irrigation/sprinkler irrigation system/agricultural machinery, irrespective of their location, subject to the following conditions:

(i) The dealer should be dealing exclusively in such items or if dealing in other products, should be maintaining separate and distinct records in respect of such items.

(ii) A ceiling of up to ₹ 30 lakh per dealer should be observed.

(l) Loans to Arthias (commission agents in rural/semi-urban areas functioning in markets/mandies) for extending credit to farmers, for supply of inputs as also for buying the output from the individual farmers/SHGs/JLGs.

(m) Credit outstanding under loans for general purposes under General Credit Cards (GCC).

(n) Loans granted to NGOs/MFIs for on-lending to individual farmers or their SHGs/JLGs.

(o) Overdrafts, up to ₹ 25,000 (per account), granted against 'no frills' accounts in rural and semi-urban areas.

1.4 Loans eligible for classification as direct/indirect finance to agriculture

(a) Credit under the Kisan Credit Card would be treated as direct finance for agriculture.

1.5 Loans not eligible for classification as direct/indirect finance to agriculture

(a) Loans sanctioned to NBFCs for on-lending to individuals or other entities against gold jewellery, investments made by banks in securitized assets originated by NBFCs, where the underlying assets are loans against gold jewellery, and purchase/assignment of gold loan portfolio from NBFCs.

ANNEXURE VII

3. Micro Credit

3.1 Loans of very small amounts not exceeding ₹ 50,000 per borrower provided by banks either directly or indirectly through a SHG/JLG mechanism for on-lending up to ₹ 50,000 per borrower.

3.2 Bank credit to Micro Finance Institutions extended on, or after, April 1, 2011 for on-lending to individuals and also to members of SHGs/JLGs will be eligible for categorization as priority sector advance under respective categories, viz., agriculture, micro and small enterprise, and micro credit (for other purposes), as indirect finance, provided not less than 85% of total assets of MFI (other than cash, balances with banks and financial institutions, government securities and money market instruments) are in the nature of "qualifying assets". In addition, aggregate amount of loan, extended for income-generating activity is not less than 75% of the total loans given by MFIs.

(a) A "qualifying asset" shall mean a loan disbursed by MFI, which satisfies the following criteria:

(i) The loan is to be extended to a borrower whose household annual income in rural areas does not exceed ₹ 60,000 while for non-rural areas it should not exceed ₹ 1,20,000.

(ii) Loan does not exceed ₹ 35,000 in the first cycle and ₹ 50,000 in the subsequent cycles.

(iii) Total indebtedness of the borrower does not exceed ₹ 50,000.

(iv) Tenure of loan is not less than 24 months when loan amount exceeds ₹ 15,000 with right to borrower of prepayment without penalty.

(v) The loan is without collateral.

(vi) Loan is repayable by weekly, fortnightly or monthly installments at the choice of the borrower.

(b) Further, the banks have to ensure that MFIs comply with the following caps on margin and interest rate as also other 'pricing guidelines' to be eligible to classify these loans as priority sector loans:

(i) Margin cap at 12% for all MFIs. The interest cost is to be calculated on average fortnightly balances of outstanding borrowings and interest income is to be calculated on average fortnightly balances of outstanding loan portfolio of qualifying assets.

(ii) Interest cap on individual loans at 26% per annum for all MFIs to be calculated on a reducing balance basis.

(iii) Only three components are to be included in pricing of loans, viz., (a) a processing fee not exceeding 1% of the gross loan amount, (b) the interest charge and (c) the insurance premium.

(iv) The processing fee is not to be included in the margin cap or the interest cap of 26%.

(v) Only the actual cost of insurance, i.e., actual cost of group insurance for life, health and livestock for borrower and spouse can be recovered; administrative charges may be recovered as per IRDA Guidelines.

(vi) There should not be any penalty for delayed payment.

(vii) No Security Deposit/Margin are to be taken.

(c) The banks should obtain from MFI at the end of each quarter, a Chartered Accountant's Certificate stating *inter alia*:

(i) 85% of total assets of the MFI are in the nature of "qualifying assets".

(ii) The aggregate amount of loan, extended for income-generating activity is not less than 75% of the total loans given by the MFIs.

(iii) Pricing guidelines are followed.

(d) The guidelines relating to categorization of:

(i) Investment by banks in securitized assets originated by MFIs.

(ii) Outright purchase of loan portfolios of MFIs as priority sector advances in the books of the banks would be issued in due course. In the meantime, fresh assets would qualify for priority sector treatment only if they satisfy the criteria of qualifying assets and adhere to the pricing guidelines as specified above.

(e) Bank loans to MFIs which do not comply with above conditions will not be reckoned as priority sector loans w.e.f. April 1, 2011. The bank loans extended prior to April 1, 2011 classified under Priority Sector will continue to be reckoned under Priority Sector till maturity of such loans.

(f) Micro Finance Institutions to be included in the above regulatory framework have to initiate requisite organizational capacity building exercise so as to enable them to conform to the above guidelines. Banks which are lending to MFIs will be one of the important pillars of the new regulatory framework and, hence they need to build up necessary criterion of due diligence while processing loan applications from MFIs. This process should be initiated immediately to ensure that MFIs availing finance from them are capable enough to put up the systems in terms of Corporate Governance, Human Resource Management, Customer Protection and other aspects or the proposed regulatory framework so as to ensure that once the new regulatory framework is in place. Micro Finance Institutions can carry out their operations without any major disruption.

3.3 Loans to poor indebted to informal sector

Loans to distressed persons (other than farmers) to prepay their debt to non-institutional lenders, against appropriate collateral or group security, would be eligible for classification under priority sector.

ANNEXURE VIII

Targets/Sub-targets

The targets and sub-targets set under priority sector lending for domestic and foreign banks operating in India are furnished below:

	Domestic Commercial Banks	**Foreign Banks**
Total Priority Sector advances	40% of Adjusted Net Bank Credit (ANBC) or credit equivalent amount of Off-balance Sheet Exposure, whichever is higher.	32% of ANBC or credit equivalent amount of Off-balance Sheet Exposure, whichever is higher.
Total agricultural advance	18% of ANBC or credit equivalent amount of Off-balance Sheet Exposure, whichever is higher.	No target.
	Of this, indirect lending in excess of 4.5% of ANBC or credit equivalent amount of Off-balance Sheet Exposure, whichever is higher will not be reckoned for computing performance under 18% target. However, all agricultural advances under the categories 'direct' and 'indirect' will be reckoned in computing performance under the overall priority sector target of 40% of ANBC or credit equivalent amount of Off-balance Sheet Exposure, whichever is higher.	
Micro and Small Enterprise (MSE) advance	Advances to micro and small enterprises sector will be reckoned in computing performance under the overall priority sector target of 40% of ANBC or credit equivalent amount of Off-balance Sheet Exposure, whichever is higher.	10% of ANBC or credit equivalent amount of Off-balance Sheet Exposure, whichever is higher.
Micro Enterprises within Micro and Small Enterprises sector	(i) 40% of total advances to micro and small enterprises sector should go to micro (manufacturing) enterprises having investment in plant and machinery up to ₹ 5 lakh and micro (service) enterprises having investment in equipment up to ₹ 2 lakh. (ii) 20% of total advances to micro and small enterprises sector should go to micro (manufacturing) enterprises with investment in plant and machinery above ₹ 5 lakh and up to ₹ 25 lakh, and micro (service) enterprises with investment in equipment above ₹ 2 lakh and up to	Same as for domestic banks.

	₹ 10 lakh. (Thus, 60% of micro and small enterprises advances should go to the micro enterprises). (iii) The increase in share of micro enterprises in MISE lending to 60% should be achieved in stages, viz., 50% in the year 2010-11, 55% in the year 2011-12 and 60% in the year 2012-13.	
Export credit	No target.	12% of ANBC or credit equivalent amount of Off-balance Sheet Exposure, whichever is higher.
Advances to weaker sections	10% of ANBC or credit equivalent amount of Off-balance Sheet Exposure, whichever is higher.	No target.
Differential Rate of Interest Scheme	1% of total advances outstanding as at the end of the previous year. It should be ensured that not less than 40% of the total advances granted under DRI scheme go to scheduled caste/scheduled tribes. At least two-third of ORI advances should be granted through rural and semi-urban branches.	No target.

ANBC or credit equivalent of Off-balance Sheet Exposures (as defined by Department of Banking Operations and Development of Reserve Bank of India from time to time) will be computed with reference to the outstanding as on March 31 of the previous year. For this purpose, outstanding FCNR(B) and NRNT deposits balances will no longer be deducted for computation of ANBC for priority sector lending purposes. For the purpose of priority sector lending, ANBC denotes NBC plus investments made by banks in non-SLR bonds held in HTM category. Investments made by banks in the Recapitalization Bonds floated by Government of India will not be taken into account for the purpose of calculation of ANBC. Existing and fresh investments, by banks in non-SLR bonds held in HTM category, will be taken into account for the purpose.. Deposits placed by banks with NABARD/SIDBI, as the case may be, in lieu of non-achievement of priority sector lending targets/sub-targets, though shown under Schedule 8 – 'Investments' in the Balance Sheet at Item I(vi) – 'Other' will not be treated as investment in non-SLR bonds held under HTM category. For the purpose of calculation of credit equivalent of Off-balance Sheet exposures, banks may use current exposure method. Interbank exposures will not be taken into account for the purpose of priority sector lending targets/sub-targets.

The net bank credit (NBC) should tally with the figures reported in the fortnightly return submitted under Section 42(2) of the Reserve Bank of India Act, 1934.

ANNEXURE IX

Financial Inclusion Plan Progress – December 2012

Sr. No.	Particulars	Year ended March 10	Year ended March 11	Year ended March 12	Progress Upto Dec. 2012
1	Total No. of Branches	85457	91145	99242	103359
2	No. of Rural Branches	33433	34811	37471	39127
3	No. of branches in unbanked villages	0	0	3381	4323
4	Total number of CSPs deployed	34532	60993	116548	152328
5	Banking Outlets > 2000 – Total	37791	66447	112130	118718
6	Banking Outlets < 2000 – Total	29903	49761	69623	92516
7	Banking Outlets – Branches	33378	34811	37471	39127
8	Banking Outlets – BCs	34174	80802	141136	168380
9	Banking Outlets – Other Modes	142	595	3146	3727
10	Banking Outlets – Total	67694	116208	181753	211234
11	Urban Locations covered through BCs	447	3771	5891	17950
12	BSBDA total (No. In lakh)	734.53	1047.59	1385.04	1714.27
13	BSBDA Total Amount (Amt. in ₹ crores)	5501.71	7612.00	12040.62	17008.35
14	OD facility availed in Basic Savings Bank Deposit A/c (No. in lakh)	1.83	6.06	27.05	32.82
15	OD facility availed in Basic Savings Bank Deposit A/c (Amt. in ₹ crores)	9.98	26.48	108.41	135.17
16	KCCs – Total – No. in lakh	243.07	271.12	302.35	317.33
17	KCCs – Total – Amt in ₹ crores	124007.06	160005.04	206839.03	249139.78
18	GCC – Total – No. in lakh	13.87	16.99	21.08	31.14
19	GCC – Total – Amt. in ₹ crores	3510.87	3507.06	4184.41	7660.35
20	ICT A/Cs – BC – Total Transaction – No. in lakhs	265.15	841.64	1410.93	1837.55
21	ICTA/Cs – BC – Total Transaction – Amt. in ₹ crores	692.07	5800.42	9285.93	16533.34

4/18/2013 20

(*Source:* Financial Inclusion and Financial Literacy PPT by Dr. Deepali Pant Joshi, ED, RBI, www.rbi.org.in)

ANNEXURE X

Part A

Details of Gross Advances, Gross NPAs, Net Advances and Net NPAs

(₹ in crores up to two decimals)

Particulars			Amount
1	Standard Advances		
2	Gross NPAs *		
3	Gross Advances ** (1 + 2)		
4	Gross NPAs as a percentage of Gross Advances (2/3) (in %)		
5	Deductions		
	(i)	Provisions held in the case of NPA Accounts as per asset classification (including additional provisions for NPAs at higher than prescribed rates)	
	(ii)	DICGC/ECGC claims received and held pending adjustment	
	(iii)	Part payment received and kept in Suspense Account or any other similar account	
	(iv)	Balance in Sundries Account (Interest Capitalization – Restructured Accounts), in respect of NPA Accounts	
	(v)	Floating Provisions***	
	(vi)	Provisions in lieu of diminution in the fair value of restructured accounts classified as NPAs	
	(vii)	Provisions in lieu of diminution in the fair value of restructured accounts classified as standard assets	
6	Net Advances (3 – 5)		
7	Net NPAs {2 – 5(i + ii + iii + iv + v + vi)}		
8	Net NPAs as percentage of Net Advances (7/6) (in %)		
	Principal dues of NPAs plus Funded Interest Term Loan (FITL) where the corresponding contra credit is parked in Sundries Account (Interest Capitalization – Restructured Accounts), in respect of NPA Accounts.		
*	For the purpose of this Statement, 'Gross Advances' mean all outstanding loans and advances including advances for which refinance has been received but excluding rediscounted bills, and advances written off at Head Office level (technical write off).		
**	Floating Provisions would be deducted while calculating Net NPAs, to the extent, banks have exercised this option, over utilizing it towards Tier-II capital.		

Part B

Supplementary Detail

(₹ in crores up to two decimals)

Particulars	Amount
Provisions on Standard Assets excluding 5(vi) in Part A above	
Interest recorded as Memorandum Item	
Amount of Cumulative Technical Write-off in respect of NPA accounts reported in Part A above	

ANNEXURE XI

DBOD BP.BC. 8/21.04.098/99 February 10, 1999

To,

All Scheduled Commercial Banks
(excluding RRBs)

Dear Sir,

Asset-Liability Management (ALM) System

1. Please refer to our circular DBOD No. BP. BC. 94/21. 04. 098/98 dated September 10, 1998 forwarding therewith draft Guidelines for putting in place Asset-Liability Manage- ment (ALM) System in banks. The draft Guidelines have been reviewed by us in the light of the issues raised/suggestions made by banks in the seminars held at Bankers' Training College and also at the Review Meeting of the Chairman/Chief Executive Officers of banks. The final Guidelines revised on the basis of the feedback received from banks are enclosed for implementation by banks effective April 1, 1999. In this connection, we have to advise as under:
2. Banks should give adequate attention to putting in place an effective ALM System. Banks should set up an internal Asset-Liability Committee (ALCO), headed by the CEO/CMD or the ED. The Management Committee or any specific Committee of the Board should oversee the implementation of the system and review its functioning periodically.
3. Keeping in view the level of computerization and the current MIS in banks, adoption of a uniform ALM System for all banks may not be feasible. The final guidelines have been formulated to serve as a benchmark for those banks which lack a formal ALM System. Banks which have already adopted more sophisticated systems may continue their existing systems but they should ensure to fine-tune their current information and reporting system so as to be in line with the ALM System suggested in the Guidelines. Other banks should examine their existing MIS and arrange to have an information system to meet the prescriptions of the new ALM System. To begin with, banks should ensure coverage of at least 60% of their liabilities and assets. As for the remaining 40% of their assets and liabilities, banks may include the position based on their estimates. It is necessary that banks set targets in the interim, for covering 100% of their business by April 1, 2000. The MIS would need to ensure that such minimum information/data consistent in quality and coverage is captured and once the ALM System stabilizes and banks gain experience, they must be in a position to switch over to more sophisticated techniques like Duration Gap Analysis, Simulation and Value at Risk for interest rate risk management.

Asset-Liability Management (ALM) System

FID. No. 38/01.02.00/98-99 April 20, 1999

To,

All-India Financial Institutions
(ICICI, IOBI, IFCI, IDFC, TFCI, IIBI,
NABARD, NHB, SIOBI and EXIM Bank)

Dear Sir,

Asset-Liability Management (ALM) System

1. As you are aware, the final guidelines tor introduction of ALM system by banks have been recently issued by RBI and the system has become operational w.e.f. April 1, 1999. Since the operations of financial institutions also give rise to liquidity and interest rate risk exposures, it has been decided to introduce an ALM system for the all-India financial institutions as well, as part of their overall system for effective risk management in their various portfolios.
2. We forward herewith the broad draft guidelines for measurement of liquidity and interest rate risk which could form the basis for evolving an ALM system by the FIs. The intention of issuing these guidelines is to sensitize the managements of FIs to the need for a formally structured management of the liquidity and interest rate risk of their portfolios and to provide a basis for initiating measures for collection, compilation and analysis of data required for an effective ALM system. The FIs may study the draft guidelines and offer their suggestions on the aspects where there are likely to be practical difficulties in implementing the guidelines latest by June 30, 1999.
3. The guidelines are expected to be particularly useful for the FIs which do not have a formal and well structured ALM system. However, if any of the FIs already have more sophisticated ALM systems in place, they may continue with the same but should fine-tune their reporting systems, where necessary, so as to continue to the prescribed guidelines. It would be desirable to constitute a small group under the charge of the senior executive responsible for treasury function of the institution, with members drawn from investments, foreign exchange, credit and MIS areas. The Group should be entrusted with the task of carrying out necessary spade work for formalizing the ALM system in the institution.
4. We would like the financial institutions to introduce the ALM system w.e.f. October 1, 1999 on a trial run basis so that they are in a position to switch over to a regular ALM system from April 1, 2000.
5. Please acknowledge receipt.

Yours faithfully,

(K.C. Bandyopadhyay)
Chief General Manager
Encl: as above

Asset-Liability Management (ALM) System in Financial Institutions (FIs) – Guidelines

In the normal course, FIs are exposed to credit and market risks in view of the asset-liability transformation. With liberalization in Indian financial markets over the last few years and growing integration of domestic markets and with external markets, the risks associated with FIs' operations have become complex and large, requiring strategic management. FIs are now operating in a fairly deregulated environment and are required to determine on their own, interest rates on deposits and advance in both domestic and foreign currencies on a dynamic basis. The interest rates on FIs' investments in government and other securities are also now market related. Intense competition for business involving both the assets and liabilities, together with increasing volatility in the domestic interest rates as well as foreign exchange rates has brought pressure on the management of FIs to maintain a good balance among spreads profitability and long-term viability. Imprudent liquidity management can put FIs' earnings and reputation at great risk. These pressures call for structured and comprehensive measures and not just ad hoc action. The management of FIs has to base their business decisions on a dynamic and integrated risk management system and process, driven by corporate strategy. FIs are exposed to several major risks in the course of their business credit risk, interest rate risk, foreign exchange risk, equity/commodity price risk, liquidity risk and operational risk. It is, therefore, important that FIs introduce effective risk management systems that address the issues related to interest rate currency and liquidity risks.

1. FIs need to address these risks in a structured manner by upgrading their risk management and adopting more comprehensive Asset-Liability Management (ALM) practices than has been done hitherto. ALM, among other functions, is also concerned with risk management and provides a comprehensive and dynamic framework for measuring, monitoring and managing liquidity, interest rate, foreign exchange and equity and commodity price risks of a bank that needs to be closely integrated with the FIs' business strategy. It involves assessment of various types of risks and altering the Asset-Liability portfolio in a dynamic way in order to manage risks.
2. This note lays down broad guidelines in respect of interest rate and liquidity risks management systems in FIs which form part of the Asset-Liability Management (ALM) function. The initial focus of the ALM function would be to enforce the risk management discipline, viz., managing business after assessing the risks involved. The objective of good risk management systems should be that these systems will evolve into a strategic tool for FIs' management.

3. The ALM process rests on three pillars:
   (i) AUM Information Systems:
   - Management Information Systems
   - Information availability, accuracy, adequacy and expediency

   (ii) ALM Organization:
   - Structure and responsibilities
   - Level of top management involvement

   (iii) ALM Process:
   - Risk parameters
   - Risk identification

   (iii) Risk measurement:
   - Risk management
   - Risk policies and tolerance levels.

4. **ALM Information Systems:** ALM has to be supported by a management philosophy which clearly specifies the risk policies and tolerance limits. This framework needs to be built on sound methodology with necessary information system as backup. Thus, information is the key to the ALM process. It is, however, recognized that varied business profiles of FIs in the public and private sector do not make the adoption of a **uniform ALM System** for all FIs feasible. There are various methods prevalent world-wide for measuring risk. These range from the simple Gap Statement to extremely sophisticated and data intensive Risk Adjusted Profitability Measurement methods. However, the central element for the entire ALM exercise is the availability of adequate and accurate information with expedience and the existing systems in many FIs do not generate information in the manner required for ALM. Collecting accurate data in a timely manner will be the biggest challenge before the FIs, particularly lacking full- scale computerization. However, the introduction of base information system for risk measurement and monitoring has to be addressed urgently. As FIs are aware internationally, regulators have prescribed or are in the process of prescribing capital adequacy for market risks. A pre-requisite for this is that FIs must have in place an efficient information system.

   Considering the large network of branches and the lack of (an adequate) support system to collect information required for ALM which analyzes information on the basis of residual maturity and behavioral pattern. It will take time for FIs in the present state to get the requisite information. In respect of foreign exchange, investment portfolio and money market operations, in view of the centralized nature of the functions, it would be much easier to collect reliable information. The data and assumptions can then be refined over time as the FI management gain experience of conducting business within an ALM framework. The spread of computerization will also help FIs in accessing data.

5. ALM Organization:

5.1 (a) Successful implementation of the risk management process would require strong commitment on the part of the senior management in the FI, to integrate basic operations and strategic decision-making with risk management. The Board should have overall responsibility for management of risks and should decide the risk management policy of the FI and set limits tor liquidity, interest rate, foreign exchange and equity price risks.

(b) The Asset-Liability Committee (ALCO) consisting of the FIs' senior management including CEO should be responsible for ensuring adherence to the limits set by the Board as well as for deciding the business strategy of the FI (on the assets and liabilities sides) in line with the FIs' budget and decided risk management objectives.

(c) The ALM Support Groups consisting of operating staff should be responsible for analyzing, monitoring and reporting the risk profiles to the ALCO. The staff should also prepare forecasts (simulations) showing the effects of various possible changes in market conditions related to the balance sheet and recommend the action needed to adhere to FIs' internal limits.

5.2 The ALCO is a decision-making unit responsible for balance sheet planning from risk return perspective including the strategic management of interest rate and liquidity risks. Each FI will have to decide on the role of its ALCO, its responsibility as also the decisions to be taken by it. The business and risk management strategy of the FI should ensure that the FI operates within the limits/parameters set by the Board. The business issues that an ALCO would consider, inter alia, will include product pricing for both deposits and advances, desired maturity profile and mix of the incremental assets and liabilities, etc. In addition to monitoring the risk levels of the FI, the ALCO should review the results of and progress in implementation of the decisions made in the previous meetings. The ALCO would also articulate the current interest rate view of the FI and base its decisions for future business strategy on this view. In respect of the funding policy, for instance, its responsibility would be to decide on source and mix of liabilities or sale of assets. Towards this end, it will have to develop a view on future direction of interest rate movements and decide on funding mixes between fixed vs. floating rate funds, wholesale vs. retail deposits, money market vs. capital market funding, domestic vs. foreign currency funding, etc. Individual FIs will have to decide the frequency for holding their ALCO meetings.

5.3 **Composition of ALCO:**

The size (number of members) of ALCO would depend on the size of each institution, business mix and organizational complexity. To ensure commitment of the Top Management and timely response to market dynamics, the CEO/CMD or the ED should head the Committee. The Chiefs of Investment, Credit, Resources Management or Planning, Funds Management/Treasury (forex and domestic), International Business and Economic Research can be members of the Committee. In addition, the Head of the Technology Division should also be an invitee for building up of MIS and related computerization. Some FIs may even have Subcommittees and Support Groups.

5.4 **Committee of Directors:**

The Management Committee of the Board or any other Specific Committee constituted by the Board should oversee the implementation of the system and review its functioning periodically.

5.5 **ALM Process:**

The scope of ALM function can be described as follows:

- Liquidity risk management
- Management of market risks
- Trading risk management
- Funding and capital planning
- Profit planning and growth projection

The guidelines given in this note mainly address Liquidity and Interest Rate risks.

6. Liquidity Risk Management:

6.1 Measuring and managing liquidity needs are vital for effective operation of FIs. By assuring a FI's ability to meet its liabilities as they become due, liquidity management can reduce the probability of an adverse situation developing. The importance of liquidity transcends individual institutions, as liquidity shortfall in one institution can have repercussions on the entire system. FIs' management should measure not only the liquidity positions of FIs on an ongoing basis but also examine how liquidity requirements are likely to evolve under different assumptions. Experience shows that assets commonly considered as liquid like Government securities and other money market instruments could also become illiquid when the market and players are unidirectional. Therefore, liquidity has to be tracked through maturity or cash flow mismatches. For measuring and managing net funding requirements, the use of a maturity ladder and calculation of cumulative surplus or deficit of funds at selected maturity dates is adopted as a standard tool. The format of the Statement of Structural Liquidity is given in Annexure I.

6.2 The Maturity Profile as given in Appendix I could be used for measuring the future cash flows of FIs in different time buckets. The time buckets, may be distributed as under:

(i) 1 to 14 days
(ii) 15 to 28 days
(iii) 29 days and upto 3 months
(iv) Over 3 months and upto 6 months
(v) Over 6 months and upto 1 year
(vi) Over I year and upto 3 years
(vii) Over 3 years and up to 5 years
(viii) Over 5 years and upto 7 years
(ix) Over 7 years and upto 10 years
(x) Over 10 years.

6.3 The investments are assumed as illiquid due to lack of depth in the secondary market and are therefore required to be shown under respective maturity buckets, corresponding to the residual maturity. However, some of the FIs may be maintaining securities in the 'Trading Book', which are kept distinct from other investments made for retaining relationship with customers. Securities held in the 'Trading Book' are subject to certain preconditions like:

(i) The composition and volume are clearly defined
(ii) Maximum maturity/duration of the portfolio is restricted
(iii) The holding period not to exceed 90 days
(iv) Cut loss limit prescribed
(v) Defeasance periods (product-wise), i.e., time taken to liquidate the position on the basis of liquidity in the secondary market are prescribed
(vi) Marking to market on a daily/weekly basis and the revaluation gain/loss charged to the profit and loss account, etc.

FIs which maintain such 'Trading Books' and complying with the above standards are permitted to show the trading securities under 1-14 days, 15-28 days and 29-90 days buckets on the basis of the defeasance periods. The Board/ALCO of the FIs should approve the volume, composition, holding/defeasance period, cut loss, etc. of the 'Trading Book' and copy of the policy note thereon should be forwarded to the Department of Banking Supervision, FID, RBI.

6.4 Within each time bucket, there could be mismatches depending on cash inflows and outflows. While the mismatches upto one year would be relevant since these provide early warning signals of impending liquidity problems, the main focus should be on the short-term mismatches, viz., 1-14 days and 15-28 days. FIs, however, are expected to monitor their cumulative mismatches (running total) across all time buckets by establishing internal prudential limits with the approval of the Board/Management Committee. The mismatches (negative gap) during 1-14 days and 15-28 days in normal course may not exceed 5% of the cash outflows in each time bucket. If a FI in view of its current asset-liability profile and the consequential structural mismatches needs higher tolerance level, it could operate with higher limit sanctioned by its Board/Management Committee giving specific reasons on the need for such higher limit. The discretion to allow a higher tolerance level is intended for a temporary period, i.e., till March 31, 2000.

6.5 The Statement of Structural Liquidity (Annexure I) may be prepared by placing all cash inflows and outflows in the maturity ladder according to the expected timing of cash flows. A maturing liability will be a cash outflow while a maturing asset will be a cash inflow. It would also be necessary to take into account the rupee inflows and outflows on account of forex operations. While determining the likely cash inflows/outflows, FIs have to make a number of assumptions according to their asset-liability profiles. While determining the tolerance levels, the FIs may take into account all relevant factors based on their asset-liability base, nature of business, future strategy, etc. The RBI is interested in ensuring that the tolerance levels are determined keeping all necessary factors in view and further refined with experience gained in Liquidity Management.

6.6 In order to enable the FIs to monitor their short-term liquidity on a dynamic basis over a time horizon spanning from 1 day to 6 months, FIs may estimate their short-term liquidity profiles on the basis of business projections and other commitments for planning purposes. An indicative format (Annexure III) for estimating Short-term Dynamic Liquidity is enclosed.

7. Currency Risk:

7.1 Floating exchange rate arrangement has brought in its wake pronounced volatility adding a new dimension to the risk profile of FIs' balance sheets. The increased capital flows across free economies following deregulation have contributed to increase in the volume of transactions. Large cross-border flows together with the volatility has rendered the FIs balance sheets vulnerable to exchange rate movements.

7.2 Dealing in different currencies brings opportunities as also risks. If the liabilities in one currency exceed the level of assets in the same currency, then the currency mismatch can add value or erode value depending upon the currency movements. The simplest way to avoid currency risk is to ensure that mismatches, if any, are reduced to zero or near zero. FIs undertake operations in foreign exchange like borrowings, making loans and advances and quoting prices for foreign exchange transactions. Irrespective of the strategies adopted, it may not be possible to eliminate currency mismatches altogether. Besides, some of the institutions may take proprietary trading positions as a conscious business strategy.

7.3 Managing Currency Risk is one more dimension of Asset-Liability Management. Mismatched currency position besides exposing the balance sheet to movements in exchange rate also exposes it to country risk and settlement risk. Following the introduction of "Guidelines for Internal Control over Foreign Exchange Business" in 1981, maturity mismatches (gaps) are also subject to control. Following the recommendations of Expert Group on Foreign Exchange Markets in India (Sodhani Committee), the calculation of exchange position has been redefined and FIs have been given the discretion to set up overnight limits linked to maintenance of capital to Risk-weighted Assets Ratio of 8% of open position limit.

7.4 Presently, the FIs are also free to set gap limits with RBI's approval but are required to adopt Value at Risk (VaR) approach to measure the risk associated with forward exposures. Thus, the open position limits together with the gap limits form the risk management approach to forex operations. For monitoring such risks, FIs should follow the instructions contained in Circular A.D. (M.A. Series) No. 52 dated December 27, 1997 issued by the Exchange Control Department.

8. Interest Rate Risk (IRR):

8.1 The phased deregulation of interest rates and the operational flexibility given to FIs in pricing most of the assets and liabilities imply the need for the financial system to hedge the Interest Rate Risk. Interest rate risk is the risk where changes in market interest rates might adversely affect a FI's financial condition. The changes in interest rates affect FIs in a larger way. The immediate impact of changes in interest rates is on FI's earnings (i.e., reported profits) by changing its Net Interest Income (Nil). A long-term impact of changing interest rates is on FI's Market Value of Equity (MVE) or Net Worth as the economic value of FI's assets, liabilities and off-balance sheet positions get affected due to variation in market interest rates. The interest rate risk when viewed from these two perspectives is known as 'earnings perspective' and 'economic value' perspective, respectively. The risk from the earnings perspective can be measured as changes in the Net Interest Income (NII) or Net Interest Margin (NIM). There are many analytical techniques for measurement and management of Interest Rate Risk. In the context of poor MIS, slow pace of computerization in FIs, the traditional gap analysis is considered as a suitable method to measure the Interest Rate Risk in the first place. It is the intention of RBI to move over to the modern techniques of Interest Rate Risk measurement like Duration Gap Analysis, Simulation and Value at Risk over time when FIs acquire sufficient expertise and sophistication in acquiring and handling MIS.

The Gap or Mismatch risk can be measured by calculating gaps over different time intervals as at a given date. Gap analysis measures mismatches between rate-sensitive liabilities and rate-sensitive assets (including off-balance sheet positions). An asset or liability is normally classified as rate sensitive if:

(i) Within the time interval under consideration, there is a cash flow

(ii) The interest rate resets/reprices contractually during the interval

(iii) Dependent on RBI changes in the interest rates/Bank Rate

(iv) It is contractually prepayable or withdrawal before the stated maturities.

8.2 The Gap Report should be generated by grouping rate-sensitive liabilities, rate-sensitive assets and off-balance sheet positions into time buckets according to residual maturity or next repricing period, whichever is earlier. The difficult task in Gap analysis is determining rate sensitivity. All investments, advances, deposits, borrowings, purchased funds, etc. that mature/reprice within a specified timeframe are interest rate sensitive. Similarly, any principal repayment of loan is also rate sensitive if the FI expects to receive it within the time horizon. This includes final principal payment and interim installments. Certain assets and liabilities receive/pay rates that vary with a reference rate. These assets and liabilities are repriced at pre-determined intervals and are rate sensitive at the time of repricing. While the interest rates on term deposits are fixed during their currency, the tranches of advances portfolio is basically floating. The interest rates on advances could be repriced any number of occasions, corresponding to the changes in PLR.

The Gaps may be identified in the following time buckets:

(i) 1-28 days

(ii) 29 days and upto 3 months

(iii) Over 3 months and upto 6 months

(iv) Over 6 months and upto 1 year

(v) Over 1 year and upto 3 years

(vi) Over 3 years and upto 5 years

(vii) Over 5 years and upto 7 years

viii) Over 7 years and upto 10 years

(ix) Over 10 years

(x) Non-sensitive

The various items of rate-sensitive assets and liabilities and off-balance sheet items may be classified as explained in Appendix II and the Reporting Format for interest rate-sensitive assets and liabilities is given in Annexure II.

8.3 The Gap is the difference between Rate-sensitive Assets (RSA) and Rate-sensitive Liabilities (RSL) for each time bucket. The positive Gap indicates that it has more RSAs than RSLs whereas the negative Gap indicates that it has more RSLs. The Gap reports indicate whether the institution is in a position to benefit from rising interest rates by having a positive Gap (RSA > RSL) or whether it is in a position to benefit from declining interest rates by a negative Gap (RSL > RSA). The Gap can, therefore be used as a measure of interest rate sensitivity.

8.4 Each FI should set prudential limits on individual Gaps with the approval of the Board/Management Committee. The prudential limits should have a relationship with the **Total Assets, Earning Assets or Equity**. The FIs may work out Earnings at Risk (EaR) or Net Interest Margin (NIM) based on their views on interest rate movements and fix a prudent level with the approval of the Board/Management Committee.

8.5 RBI will also introduce capital adequacy for market risks in due course.

9. General:

9.1 The classification of various components of assets and liabilities into different time buckets for preparation of Gap reports (Liquidity and Interest Rate Sensitivity) as indicated in Appendices I and II is the **benchmark**. FIs which are better equipped to reasonably estimate the behavioral pattern, embedded options, rolls-in and rolls-out, etc. of various components of assets and liabilities on the basis of past data/empirical studies could classify them in the appropriate time buckets, subject to approval from the ALCO/Board. A copy of the note approved by the ALCO/Board may be sent to the Department of Banking Supervision, Financial Institutions Division.

9.2 The present framework does not capture the impact of embedded options, i.e., the customers exercising their options (premature closure of deposits, bonds and prepayment of loans and advances) on the liquidity and interest rate risks profile of FIs. The magnitude of embedded option risk at times of volatility in market interest rates is quite substantial. FIs should, therefore, evolve suitable mechanism, supported by empirical studies and behavioral analysis to estimate the future behavior of assets, liabilities and off-balance sheet items to changes in market variables and estimate the embedded options.

9.3 A scientifically evolved internal transfer pricing model by assigning values on the basis of current market rates to funds provided and funds used is an important component for effective implementation of ALM System. The transfer price mechanism can enhance the management of margin, i.e., lending or credit spread, the funding or liability spread and mismatch spread. It also helps centralizing interest rate risk at one place which facilitate effective control and management of interest rate risk. A well-defined transfer pricing system also provide a rational framework for pricing of assets and liabilities.

ANNEXURE XII

Gap Statement

	day 1	2 to 7 days	8 to 14 days	15 to 28 days	29 days to 3 months	Over 3 months to 6 months	Over 6 months to 1 year	Over 1 years to 3 years	Over 3 years to 5 years	Over 5 years	Total
Outflows											
Capital										500	500
Reserves and Surplus										1250	1250
Demand Deposits	750	50	0	0	0	0	0	7050	0	0	7850
Time Deposits	0	0	1000	1200	500	400	750	3000	1000	1300	9150
Borrowings	0	0	200	100	0	0	50	0	0	0	350
Other Liabilities	0	0	200	0	0	570	0	0	0	800	1570
Commited Lines	50	0	0	0	0	0	0	0	0	0	50
L/C, B/G	0	0	10	10	10	20	20	10	10	10	100
Total Outflows	800	50	1410	1310	510	990	820	10060	1010	3860	20820
Inflows											
Cash	0	0	60	0	0	0	0	0	0	0	60
Bal with RBI	450	50	0	0	0	100	40	300	0	560	1500
Bal with Other banks	400	0	0	0	0	0	100	200	0	0	700
Investments	0	0	500	920	320	360	500	200	200	1000	4000
Advances	0	0	2000	2000	750	500	500	2000	1000	5000	13750
NPAs	0	0	0	0	0	0	0	0	250	0	250
Fixed Assets	0	0	0	0	0	0	0	0	0	250	250
Other Assets	0	0	40	20	30	30	25	15	0	0	160
Total Inflows	850	50	2600	2940	1100	990	1165	2715	1450	6810	20670
Mismatch (I-O)	50	0	1190	1630	590	0	345	-7345	440	2950	-150
Cumulative Mismatch	50	50	1240	2870	3460	3460	3805	-3540	-3100	-150	-150

Note: As per present guidelines, negative mismatches (inflow – outflow) during first 28 days should not exceed outflows by 5% in 1 day, 10% in 2-7 days, 15% in 8-14 days, 20% in 15-28 days time bucket. For rest of the time buckets, individual banks may decide its own prudential norms.

ANNEXURE XIII

Bank X is expecting increase in loans and advances to the extent of ₹ 2300 crores in the next quarter. Bank wants to invest in Government Securities to the extent of ₹ 700 in the next 90 days. Redemption will take place after 6 months. Bank is expecting growth of deposits of around ₹ 1350 crores in the next quarter. CRR is 4%. Excess CRR of ₹ 50 crores is maintained. Prepare a Short-term Dynamic Liquidity Statement.

Short-term Dynamic Liquidity Statement

	1 day	2-7 days	8-14 days	15-28 days	29 days to 3 months
Outflows					
Increase in Loans and Advances	100	200	200	300	1500
Net Increase in Investments	50	50	150	150	300
Inter-bank obligations (Off-balance Sheet Items)	500	300	1000	200	700
Others	100	100	100	100	300
Total (A)	750	650	1450	750	2800
Inflows					
Net cash position (Mandatory CRR @ 4% on deposit growth of ₹ 1350 crores + excess CRR of ₹ 50 crores **Note:** CRR of ₹ 54 crores not shown as inflows as it is mandatory	50	50	50	50	50
Net increase in deposits	150	200	350	150	500
Term Deposits	80	120	280	100	400
Demand Deposits	70	80	70	50	100
Redemptions				300	100
Repos, Swaps, Bill Discounted	2000	1500	3050	350	1450
Total (B)	2200	1750	3450	850	2100
Mismatch (B – A)	1450	1100	2000	100	–700

Note: Liquidity position is comfortable in the first four buckets. In the fifth bucket, mismatch (-700) exceeds total outflows (2800) by 25%. For the first four buckets, regulators' prudential guidelines provide mismatch not to exceed 5%, 10%, 15% and 25% respectively. In the fifth bucket, i.e., 29 days-3 months banks' own approved prudential norms are 25%. Hence, here the mismatch is within approved norms.

ANNEXURE XIV

Gap and Net Interest Income

Balance Sheet for Wonderful Bank:

	Assets	Yield	Liabilities	Cost
Rate-sensitive	₹ 600	7%	₹ 700	4%
Fixed Rate	₹ 450	10%	₹ 300	5%
Non-performing	₹ 250		₹ 150	
			₹ 1,150	
			Equity	
			₹ 150	
Total	₹ 1,300		₹ 1,300	

$NII = (0.07 \times 600 + 0.10 \times 450) - (0.04 \times 700 + 0.05 \times 300)$

$NII = 87 - 43 = 44$

$NIM = 44/1050 = 4.19\%$

$GAP = 600 - 700 = -100$

[Net Interest Income (NII) = Interest Income – Interest Expenses.

Net Interest Margin (NIM) = NII/Performing Assets]

ANNEXURE XV

Gap-NII Relationship

GAP Summary

Gap	**Change in Interest Income**	**Change in Interest Income**		**Change in Interest Expense**	**Change in Net Interest Income**
Positive	Increase	Increase	>	Increase	Increase
Positive	Decrease	Decrease	>	Decrease	Decrease
Negative	Increase	Increase	<	Increase	Decrease
Negative	Decrease	Decrease	<	Decrease	Increase
Zero	Increase	Increase	=	Increase	None
Zero	Decrease	Decrease	=	Decrease	None

ANNEXURE XVI

1% Increase in Rates

Balance Sheet for Wonderful Bank

	Assets	Rate	Liabilities	Cost
Rate-sensitive	₹ 600	8%	₹ 700	5%
Fixed Rate	₹ 450	10%	₹ 300	5%
Non-performing	₹ 250		₹ 150	
			₹ 1,150	
			Equity	
			₹ 150	
Total	₹ 1,300		₹ 1,300	

NII = (0.08 × 600 + 0.10 × 450) – (0.05 × 700 + 0.05 × 300)

NII = 93 – 50 = 43

NIM = 43/1050 = 4.09%

GAP = 600 – 700 = –100

[When the GAP is negative, more liabilities will reprice higher than assets. Hence, NII and NIM fall with increase in rates. Effects of change in NII in positive and negative gaps are given in Annexure XV].

ANNEXURE XVII

Progress of Commercial Banking at a Glance

Important Indicators	June 1969	March 2003	March 2004	March 2005	March 2006	March 2007	March 2008	March 2009	March 2010	March 2011
	1	2	3	4	5	6	7	8	9	10
No. of Commercial Banks	89	294	291	288	222	183	175	170	169	169
Scheduled Commercial Banks	73	289	286	284	218	179	171	166	165	165
of which: Regional Rural Banks	–	196	196	196	133	96	91	86	82	82
Non-scheduled Commercial Banks	16	5	5	4	4	4	4	4	4	4
Number of Offices of Scheduled Commercial Banks in India ^	8262	66535	67188	68355	69471	71839	76050	80547	85393	90263
(a)Rural	1833	32303	32121	32082	30579	30551	31076	31667	32624	33683
(b)Semi-urban	3342	14859	15091	15403	15556	16361	17675	18969	20740	22843
(c) Urban	1584	10693	11000	11500	12032	12970	14391	15733	17003	17490
(d)Metropolitan	1503	8680	8976	9370	11304	11957	12908	14178	15026	16247
Population per Office (in thousands)	64.0	16.0	16.0	16.0	16.0	15.0	15.0	14.5	13.8	13.4
Deposits of Scheduled Commercial Banks in India (₹ Billion)	46.46	13117.61#	15422.84&	17328.58&	21090.49	26119.33	31969.39	38341.10	44928.26	52079.69
of which: (a) Demand	21.04	1878.37	2459.43	2650.33	3646.40	4297.31	5243.10	5230.85	6456.10	6417.05
(b) Time	25.42	11239.24	12963.42	14678.24	17444.09	21822.03	26726.30	33110.25	38472.16	45662.64
Credit of Scheduled Commercial Banks in India (₹ Billion)	35.99	7464.32	8655.94	11243.00	15070.77	19311.89	23619.14	27755.49	32447.88	39420.82
Deposits of Scheduled Commercial Banks per Office (₹ Million)	5.6	197.2	229.5	253.5	303.6	363.1	420.4	476.0	526.1	577.0
Credit of Scheduled Commercial Banks per Office (₹ Million)	4.4	112.2	128.8	164.5	216.9	268.5	310.6	344.6	380.0	436.7
Per Capita Deposits of Scheduled Commercial Banks (₹)	88	12554	14550	16091	19276	23468	28327	33471	38062	43034
Per Capita Credit of Scheduled Commercial Banks (₹)	68	7143	8166	10440	13774	17355	20928	24230	27489	32574
Deposits of Scheduled Commercial Banks as Percentage of National Income (at Current Prices)	15.5	65.3	68.5	68.5	73.8	79.1	84.4	88.1	86.6	82.3
Scheduled Commercial Banks' Advances to Priority Sector (₹ Billion)	5.04	2509.89	3113.35	4007.75	5467.74	7037.59	8247.73	9674.14	11384.06	13373.33
Share of Priority Sector Advances in Total Credit of Scheduled Commercial Banks (per cent)	14.0	34.6	37.1	36.7	37.2	36.5	34.9	34.8	35.1	33.9
Share of Priority Sector Advances in Total Non-food	15.0	37.1	38.8	38.1	38.2	37.4	35.6	35.4	35.6	34.5

Credit of Scheduled Commercial Banks (per cent)										
Credit Deposit Ratio	77.5	56.9	56.1	64.9	71.5	73.9	73.9	72.4	72.2	75.7
Investment Deposit Ratio	29.3	41.3	43.8	41.6	35.5	30.3	30.4	30.4	30.8	28.8
Cash Deposit Ratio	8.2	8.3	5.6	6.9	6.6	7.5	8.6	6.7	6.8	6.7

#: Includes Resurgent India Bonds (RIB) (₹ 179.45 Billion) and also India Millennium Deposits (IMD) (₹256.62 Billion)

&: Includes India Millennium Deposits (IMD) (₹ 256.62 Billion)

^: Excludes Administrative Offices

See Notes on Tables.

ANNEXURE XVIII

Consolidated Balance Sheet of Scheduled Commercial Banks

(Amount in ₹ billion)

Item	As at end-March 2012							
	Public sector banks	SBI group	Nationalised banks*	Private sector banks	Old private sector banks	New private sector banks	Foreign banks	All scheduled commercia l banks
1	2	3	4	5	6	7	8	9
1. Capital	183	12	171	48	13	35	406	637
2. Reserves and Surplus	3,373	1,061	2,312	1,545	266	1,279	531	5,449
3. Deposits	50,020	14,050	35,970	11,746	3,159	8,587	2,771	64,537
3.1 Demand Deposits	3,844	1,197	2,647	1,659	258	1,401	801	6,303
3.2 Savings Banks Deposits	12,140	4,537	7,604	2,729	578	2,152	419	15,289
3.3 Term Deposits	34,036	8,317	25,719	7,358	2,323	5,035	1,551	42,945
4. Borrowings	4,618	1,588	3,030	2,584	198	2,386	1,199	8,401
5. Other Liabilities and Provisions	2,186	1,002	1,184	855	114	741	929	3,970
Total Liabilities/Assets	60,380	17,712	42,668	16,778	3,750	13,028	5,836	82,994
1. Cash and Balances with RBI	2,800	791	2,009	706	167	538	232	3,737
2. Balances with Banks and Money at Call and Short Notice	1,760	482	1,278	366	71	295	312	2,437
3. Investments	15,041	4,173	10,868	5,260	1,093	4,166	2,005	22,305
3.1 Government Securities (a + b)	12,580	3,513	9,067	3,474	785	2,688	1,376	17,429
(a) In India	12,494	3,494	9,000	3,468	785	2,683	1,376	17,338
(b) Outside India	85	19	67	5.6	–	5.6	–	91
3.2 Other Approved Securities	10	0.2	9.7	0.2	0.2	0.01	–	10
3.3 Non-approved Securities	2,451	660	1791	1,786	308	1,478	629	4,866
4. Loans and Advances	38,783	11,520	27,263	9,664	2,301	7,363	2,298	50,746
4.1 Bills Purchased and Discounted	2,307	888	1,419	357	113	244	257	2,922
4.2 Cash Credits, Overdrafts, etc.	16,085	4,958	11,127	2,860	1,120	1,740	1,099	20,044
4.3 Term Loans	20,391	5,674	14,717	6,447	1,068	5,380	942	27,780
5. Fixed Assets	383	74	309	134	27	107	50	567
6. Other Assets	1,613	672	941	649	91	558	939	3,201

Note: Nil/negligible. Components may not add up to their respective totals due to rounding off numbers to ₹ billion

*: Includes IDBI Bank Ltd

(***Source:*** Annual accounts of respective banks.)

(***Source:*** Report on Trend and Progress of Banking in India 2011-12, Operations and Performance of Commercial Banks)

ANNEXURE XIX

Bank Group-wise Deposits of Scheduled Commercial Banks According to Type Deposits March 2011

(No. of Accounts in Thousands, Amount in ₹ Million)

Bank Group	Current		Savings		Term		Total	
	No. Of Accounts	Amount	No. of Accounts	Amount	No. of Accounts	Amount	No. of Accounts	Amount
	1	2	3	4	5	6	7	8
State Bank of India and its Associates	3,833 (1.9)	1218710.9 (10.6)	165,421 (80.8)	4033058.5 (34.9)	35,561 (17.4)	6288438.6 (54.5)	204,814 (100.0)	11540207.9 (100.0)
Nationalised Banks	21,776 (5.4)	3168200.2 (11.1)	304,959 (75.3)	7037605.2 (24.6)	78,360 (19.3)	18443435.2 (64.4)	405,095 (100.0)	28649240.5 (100.0)
Foreign Banks	302 (7.6)	710784.5 (30.3)	2,924 (73.9)	398147.4 (17.0)	730 (18.5)	1238673.2 (52.8)	3,956 (100.0)	2347605.1 (100.0)
Regional Rural Banks	1,695 (1.6)	83422.1 (5.1)	92,855 (85.6)	902789.8 (55.2)	13,890 (12.8)	650733.3 (39.8)	108,441 (100.0)	1636945.3 (100.0)
Private Sector Banks	11,555 (13.2)	1520148.3 (15.6)	57,838 (65.9)	2290515.9 (23.6)	18,430 (21.0)	5910850.4 (60.8)	87,823 (100.0)	9721514.5 (100.0)
All Scheduled Commercial Banks	39,161 (4.8)	6701266.0 (12.4)	623,997 (77.0)	14662116.6 (27.2)	146,971 (18.1)	32532130.6 (60.4)	810,129 (100.0)	53895513.3 (100.0)

ANNEXURE XX

Trend in Growth of Banking Assets

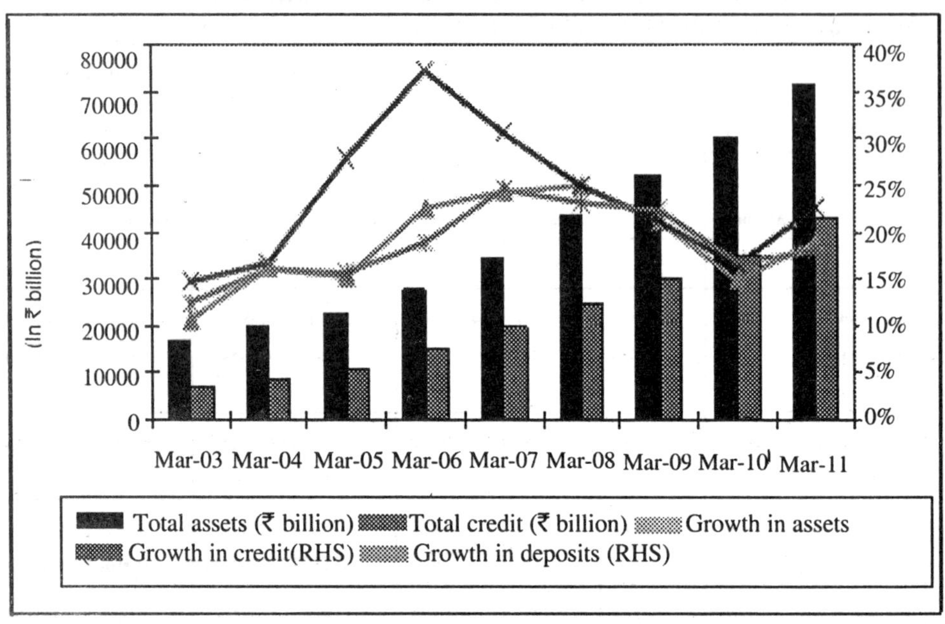

(*Source:* RBI, ICRA Research)

Domestic Credit Portfolio Composition of Scheduled Commercial Banks

Credit Portfolio Composition	March 25, 2010	March 25, 2011	As % of Total Credit as in March 2011	Growth (y-o-y)
Agriculture and Allied Activities loans	4,161	4,603	13%	11%
Non-agriculture Corporate Loans				
Commercial Real Estate Loans	921	1,118	3%	21%
Loans to NBFCs	1,134	1,756	5%	55%
Power Sector Loans	1,878	2,692	7%	43%
Other Infrastructure Loans	1,920	2,575	7%	34%
Other Corporate Loans	14,528	17,076	47%	18%
Retail Loans				
Housing Loans	3,009	3,461	9%	15%
Credit Card Outstanding	201	181	0%	10%
Vehicle Loans	638	793	2%	24%
Other Retail Loans	2,008	2,419	7%	20%
Total Non-food Credit	30,400	36,674	100%	21%

Note: Amounts in ₹ billion y-o-y: year-on-year

(*Source*: RBI, ICRA Research)

ANNEXURE XXI

Targets and Sub-targets for PSL

Categories	Domestic commercial banks/Foreign banks with 20 and above branches	Foreign banks with less than 20 branches
Total Priority Sector	40% of Adjusted Net Bank Credit (ANBC) or credit equivalent amount of Off-balance Sheet Exposure (CEOBE), whichever is higher.	32% of ANBC or CEOBE, whichever is higher.
Total Agriculture	18% of ANBC or CEOBE, whichever is higher. Of this, indirect lending in excess of 4.5% of ANSC or CEOSE, whichever is higher, will not be reckoned for computing achievement under 18% target. However, all agricultural loans under the categories 'direct' and 'indirect' will be reckoned in computing achievement under the overall priority sector target of 40% of ANBC or credit equivalent amount of off-balance Sheet Exposure, whichever is higher.	No specific target. Forms part of total priority sector target.
Micro and Small Enterprises (MSEs)	(i) Advances to micro and small enterprises sector will be reckoned in computing achievement under the overall priority sector target of 40% of ANBC or CEOBE, whichever is higher. (ii) 40% of total advances to micro and mall enterprises sector should go to Micro (manufacturing) enterprises having investment in plant and machinery up to ₹ 5 lakh and micro (service) enterprises having investment in equipment up to ₹ 2 lakh. (iii) 20% of total advances to micro and small enterprises sector should go to Micro (manufacturing) enterprises with investment in plant and machinery above ₹ 5 lakh and up to ₹ 25 lakh, and micro (service) enterprises with investment in equipment above ₹ 2 lakh and up to ₹ 10 lakh.	No specific target. Forms part of total priority sector target.
Export Credit	Export credit is not a separate category. Export credit to eligible activities under agriculture and MSE will be reckoned for priority sector lending under respective categories.	No specific target. Forms part of total priority sector target.
Advance to Weaker Sections	10% of ANBC or CEOBE, whichever is higher.	No specific target. Forms part of total priority sector target.

Note: For foreign banks with 20 and above branches, priority sector targets and sub-targets have to be achieved within a maximum period of five years starting from April 1, 2013 and ending on March 31, 2018. Foreign banks with 20 and above branches will submit an action plan latest by December 31, 2012 for achieving the targets over a specific timeframe to be approved by RBI.

(***Source:*** http://financialservices.gov.in/banking/PSL%20Note.pdf)

ANNEXURE XXII

Progress under Financial Inclusion Plans

Sr. No.	Particulars	As on March 2011	As on March 2012
1	2	3	4
1	Total number of Customer Service Points deployed	60,993	16,548
2	Total banking outlets in villages, of which: (i) Branches (ii) BCs (iii) Other modes	1,16,208 34,811 80,802 595	1,81,753 37,471 1,41,136 3146
3	Urban locations covered through BCs	3,771	5,891
4	ICT-based A/Cs – through BCs (No. in Mill- ion)	32	57
5	ICT-based A/Cs – transactions (No. in Mill- ion)	84	141
6	ICT-based A/CS – transactions (Amount in Billion)	58	93
7	Number of No-frills Accounts (in Million)	105	139
8	Amount of No-frills Account (₹ Billion)	76	120
9	Number of No-frills Accounts with OD (in Million)	0.6	2.7
10	Amount in No-frills A/Cs with OD (₹ Billion)	0.3	1.1
11	Number of KCCs Outstanding (in Million)	27	30
12	Amount in KCCs Outstanding (₹ Billion)	1,600	2,068
13	Number of GCCs Outstanding (in Million)	1.7	2.1
14	Amount in GCCs Outstanding (₹ Billion)	35	42

(*Source:* Report on Trend and Progress of Banking in India 2011-12, Operations and Performance of Commercial Banks)

Progress of Micro-finance Programmes

(As at end-March)

Item	Self-help Group					
	Number (in million)			Amount (₹ billion)		
	2009-10	2010-11	2011-12P	2009-10	2010-11	2011-12P
Loans disbursed by bank	1.5 (0.27)	1.2 (0.2)	1.1 (0.2)	145 (22)	145 (25)	165 (26)
Loans outstanding with banks	4.8 (1.3)	4.8 (1.3)	4.4 (1.2)	280 (63)	312 (78)	363 (80.5)
Saving with banks	6.9 (1.7)	7.5 (2.0)	8.0 (2.1)	62 (13)	70 (18)	66 (14)
Item	**Micro-finance Institutions**					
	Number (in million)			**Amount (₹ billion)**		
	2009-10	**2010-11**	**2011-12P**	**2009-10**	**2010-11**	**2011-12P**
Loans disbursed by bank	691	469	465	81	76	52
Loans outstanding with banks	1,513	2,176	1,960	101	107	115

***Note*:** 1. Figures in brackets indicate the details about SHGs covered under Swarnjayanti Gram Swarozgar Yojana (SGSY).

2. P: Provisional data.

(***Source:*** NABARD).

(***Source:*** Report on Trend and Progress of Banking in India 2011-12, Operations and Performance of Commercial Banks.)

ANNEXURE XXIII

Trend in Asset Quality Indicators of SCBs

SCBs	**FY06**	**FY07**	**FY08**	**FY09**	**FY10**	**FY11**
Gross NPAs (%)	3.3	2.5	2.3	2.3	2.4	2.3
Net NPAs (%)	1.2	1.0	1.0	1.1	1.1	0.9
Fresh NPA Generation Rate (%)	2.0	1.7	1.8	2.1	2.2	2.0
Net NPAs/Net Worth (%)	10.1	9.2	7.8	8.6	9.1	10.0
PSBs	**FY06**	**FY07**	**FY08**	**FY09**	**FY10**	**FY11**
Gross NPAs (%)	3.6	2.7	2.2	2.0	2.2	2.3
Net NPAs (%)	1.3	1.1	1.0	0.9	1.1	1.1
Net NPAs/Net Worth (%)	13.1	12.1	11.2	11.4	13.5	13.4
Private Banks	**FY06**	**FY07**	**FY08**	**FY09**	**FY10**	**FY11**
Gross NPAs (%)	2.1	2.1	2.4	2.9	2.7	2.3
Net NPAs (%)	0.9	0.9	1.1	1.3	1.0	0.6
Net NPAs/Net Worth (%)	6.3	7.8	6.1	7.5	5.3	3.2

(***Source:*** Annual Reports of Banks, RBI, ICRA Research)

(***Source:*** www.icra.in. Research 2011)

- Over the last two years, PSBs "Gross NPAs rose from 2% to 2.3%, while private banks' NPAs declined from 2.9% to 2.3%. The Gross NPA percentage of the PSBs got impacted by slippages from restructured accounts, "agri debt relief", and slippages because of automation of asset classification.
- Better provisioning coverage and a stronger capitalisation profile allowed private banks report better solvency (Net NPAs/Net Worth) than PSBs during last few years.

ANNEXURE XXIV

Composition of NPAs of Public Sector Banks – 2003 to 2012

(Amount in ₹ Billion)

Bank Group/Years	As on March 31						
	Priority Sector		Non-priority Sector		Public Sector		Total
	Amount	% Share	Amount	% Share	Amount	% Share	Amount
	(1)	(2)	(3)	(4)	(5)	(6)	(7)
A. Nationalised Banks							
2003	168.86	47.10	184.02	51.33	5.61	1.56	358.49
2004	167.05	47.74	178.95	51.14	3.90	1.11	349.90
2005	163.80	49.81	162.25	49.33	2.83	0.86	328.88
2006	151.24	53.66	122.53	43.48	8.08	2.87	281.85
2007	157.79	61.28	96.68	37.55	3.02	1.17	257.49
2008	163.85	67.21	77.93	31.96	2.02	0.83	243.80
2009	157.21	60.09	101.44	38.77	2.97	1.14	261.62
2010	199.06	56.13	152.77	43.08	2.80	0.79	354.63
2011	257.21	59.90	169.47	39.47	2.73	0.64	429.41
2012	322.90	48.34	334.87	50.13	1.92	0.29	659.69
B. Nationalised Banks							
2003	80.53	47.49	83.79	49.41	5.26	3.10	169.58
2004	71.36	47.07	78.03	51.47	2.20	1.45	151.59
2005	70.17	47.39	76.24	51.49	1.68	1.13	148.09
2006	72.50	54.95	58.19	44.11	1.25	0.95	131.94
2007	71.75	57.14	51.93	41.36	1.88	1.50	125.56
2008	89.02	58.49	62.22	40.88	0.97	0.64	152.21
2009	84.47	47.26	92.50	51.75	1.77	0.99	178.74
2010	109.40	50.11	106.46	48.77	2.44	1.12	218.30
2011	155.67	55.32	125.67	44.66	0.06	0.02	281.40
2012	239.11	52.33	217.59	47.62	0.25	0.05	456.95
Public Sector Banks (A + B)							
2003	249.39	47.23	267.81	50.71	10.87	2.06	528.07
2004	238.41	47.54	256.98	51.24	6.10	1.22	501.49
2005	233.97	49.05	238.49	50.00	4.51	0.95	476.97
2006	223.74	54.07	180.72	43.68	9.33	2.25	413.79
2007	229.54	59.92	148.61	38.80	4.90	1.28	383.05
2008	252.87	63. 8 6	140.15	35.39	2.99	0.76	369.01
2009	241.68	54 .88	193.94	44.04	4.74	1.08	440.36
2010	308.46	53.84	25 9.23	45.25	5.24	0.91	572.93
2011	412.88	58.09	29 5.14	41.52	2.79	0.39	710.81
2012	562.01	49.96	552.46	49.11	2.17	0.19	1116.64

(***Source:*** Off-site Returns (Domestic and Provisional of Banks, Department of Banking Supervision, RBI)

APPENDIX I

Maturity Profile – Liquidity

Heads of Accounts Time Bucket Category

A. Outflows	
1. Capital funds: (a) Equity capital, Non-redeemable or perpetual preference capital. Reserves, Funds and Surplus (b) Preference capital – redeemable/non-perpetual	The 10 year and above time bucket. As per the residual maturity of the shares. The 10 year and above time bucket. However, if such gifts, grants, etc., are tied to specific end-use, then these may be slotted in the time bucket as per purpose/end-use specified.
2. Gifts, grants, donations and benefactions	
3. Notes, Bonds and Debentures: (including Subordinated bonds, rupee as well as foreign currency bonds the proceeds of which have been con vetted into rupees) (a) Plain vanilla bonds/debentures (b) Bonds/debentures with embedded call/put options (including zero coupon/deep discount bonds) (c) Fixed rate notes	 As per the residual maturity of the instruments. As per the residual period for the earliest exercise date for the embedded option. As per the residual maturity.
4. Deposits: (a) Term deposits from public	 As per the residual maturity. Alternatively, the FIs which are better equipped, could analyze the behavior of their deposits in terms of exercise of

	embedded options subject to lock-in period, roll-in and roll-out of deposits, etc., and slot them as per their behavioral maturity rather than the residual maturity.
(b) Inter-corporate Deposits	These being institutional/wholesale deposits, should be slotted as per their residual maturity.
(c) Certificates of Deposit	As per the residual maturity.
5. Borrowings:	
(a) Term money borrowings	As per the residual maturity
(b) From RBI, Government and others	-do-
6. Current liabilities and provisions:	
(a) Sundry creditors	As per the due date or likely timing of cash outflows. A behavioral analysis could also be made to assess the trend of outflows and the amounts slotted accordingly.
(b) Expenses payable (other than interest)	As per the likely time of cash outflow.
(c) Advance income received receipts from borrowers pending adjustment	In the '10 year and above' time bucket as these do not involve any cash outflow.
(d) Interest payable on bonds/deposits	In respective time buckets as per the due date of payment, the amount of interest overdue (including the amount pre-funded in the account with RBI for servicing of outstanding SLR bonds pending claims from investors) be shown in 1-14 days time bucket. In case of floating rate bonds/deposits, outflow may be calculated at current interest rate.
(e) Provisions for NPAs	The amount of provision may be netted out from the gross amount of the NPA portfolio and the net amount of NPAs be shown as an item under inflows in stipulated time buckets.
(f) Provisions for investment portfolio	The amount may be netted from the gross value of investments portfolio and the net investments be shown as inflow in the prescribed time slots. In case provisions are not held security-wise, the provision may be shown on "over 10 years bucket".
(g) Other provisions	To be bucketed as per the purpose/nature of the underlying transaction.
B. Inflows	
1. Cash	In 1 to 14 days time-bucket.
2. Remittance in transit	-do-

3. Balance with RBI	-do-
4. Balance with banks (in India only):	
(a) Current account:	The stipulated minimum balance be shown in 1 to 3 years bucket. The balance in excess of the minimum balance be shown in 1 to 14 days time bucket.
(b) Money at call and short notice	In 1 to 14 days time bucket.
(c) Deposit accounts/short-term deposits	As per residual maturity.
5. Investments (net of provisions):	
(a) Government securities	As per residual maturity of the securities.
(b) Corporate bonds and debentures	As per residual maturity of the instruments. However, the bonds/debentures valued by applying NPA norms due to non-servicing of interest, should be shown in 3-5 years bucket if substandard norms and in 5 to 7 years bucket if doubtful norms are applied for valuation respective.
(c) Non-convertible, redeemable preference shares and units of closed-ended mutual funds	As per residual maturity of the instruments.
(d) Equity shares, convertible preference shares, non-redeemable, perpetual pre- ference shares, shares of subsidiaries/joint ventures and units in open ended mutual funds	(i) Shares classified as "current" investments representing trading book of the FI may be shown in time buckets of 1-14 days. 15-28 days and 29 days to upto 3 months time buckets as per the defeasance period (i.e., the time required to liquidate these shares) of various securities. (ii) Shares classified as "long-term" investments may be kept in 10 year and above bucket. However, the shares of the assisted units/companies acquired as part of the initial financing package, may be slotted in the relative time bucket keeping in view the pace of project implementation/time overrun, etc., and the resultant likely timeframe for divesting such shares.
(e) Venture capital units	In the 10 years and above time bucket.
6. Advance (Performing):	
(a) Bill of Exchange and promissory notes discounted and rediscounted.	As per the residual usance of the underlying bills.
(b) Term loans (rupee loans only)	The cash inflows on account of the interest and principal of the loan may be slotted in respective time buckets as per the timing of the cash flows as stipulated

	in the original/revised repayment schedule.
(c) Corporate loans/short term loans.	As per the residual maturity.
7. Non-performing: Non-performing loans (may be shown net of the provisions, interest suspense held and the amount of claims received from ECGC).	
(a) Substandard:	
(i) All overdues and installments of principal falling due during the next three years	In the 3 to 5 years time bucket.
(ii) Entire principal amount due beyond the next three years	In the time bucket arrived at after adding 3 years to the respective due dates of various installments of principal.
(b) Doubtful and loss:	
(i) All installments of principal falling due during the next five years as also all overdues	In the 3 to 5 years time bucket.
(ii) Entire principal amount due beyond the next five years	In the time bucket arrived at after adding 3 years to the respective due dates of various installments of principal.
8. Assets on lease	Cash flows from the lease transaction may be slotted in respective time buckets as per the timing of the cash flow.
9. Fixed assets (excluding leased assets)	In the 10 years and above time bucket.
10. Other assets	
(a) Intangible assets and items not representing cash inflows.	In the 10 years and above time bucket.
(b) Other items (such as accrued income, other receivables, staff loans. etc.).	In respective maturity buckets as per the timing of the cash flows.
C. Contingent liabilities:	
(a) Letters of credit/guarantees (outflow through devolvement)	Based on the past trend analysis of the devolvements *vis-à-vis* the outstanding amount of LCs/guarantees (net of margins held), the like devolvements should be estimated and this amount could be distributed in various time buckets on judgmental basis. The assets create out of devolvements may be shown under respective maturity buckets on the basis of probable recovery dates.
(b) Loan commitments pending disbursal (outflow)	In the respective time buckets as per the sanctioned disbursement schedule.
(c) Lines of credit committed to/by other Institutions (outflow/inflow)	In 1 to 14 days time bucket.

(d) Underwriting commitments (outflow)	Based on the analysis of the past trend of devolvement of underwriting commitments, amount of such commitments may be slotted the relative time bucket as per the time schedt of IPO/finalisation of allotment.
(e) Forward exchange contracts/rupee dollar swaps, bills rediscounted and repos (inflow/outflow)	In the respective time buckets as per the residual maturity of the underlying bills/transactions.

Notes:

(a) Any event-specific cash flows (e.g., outflow due to wage settlement arrears, capital expenses, income tax refunds, etc.) should be shown in a time bucket corresponding to timing of such cash flows.

(b) All overdue liabilities be shown in the 1 to 14 days time bucket.

(c) Overdue receivables on account of interest and installments of standard loans should be slotted as below:

(i) Overdue for less than one month	In 3 to 6 months bucket.
(ii) Interest overdue for more than one month but less than seven months (i.e., before the relative amount becomes past due tor six months)	In 6 to 12 months bucket without reckoning the grace period of one month.
(iii) Principal installments overdue for 7 months but less than one year	In 1 to 3 years bucket.

D. Financing of Gaps:

The negative gap (i.e., where outflows exceed inflows) in the 1 to 14 days and 15-28 days time bucket should not exceed the prudential limit of 5% of outflows of each time bucket and the cumulative gap upto the one year period should not exceed 10% of the cumulative cash outflows upto one year period. In case these limits are exceeded, the measures proposed for bringing the gaps within the limit, should be shown by a footnote in the relative statement.

APPENDIX II

Interest Rate Sensitivity

Heads of Accounts	Rate Sensitivity of Time Bucket
Liabilities	
1. Capital, Reserves and Surplus	Non-sensitive
2. Gifts, grants and benefactions	-do-
3. Notes, bonds and debentures	
(a) Floating rate	Sensitive reprice on the rollover/repricing date should be slotted in respective time buckets as per the repricing dates.
(b) Fixed rate (plain vanilla) including zero coupons	Sensitive; reprice on maturity. To be placed in respective time buckets as per the residual maturity of such instruments.
(c) Instruments with embedded options	Sensitive could reprice on the exercise date of the option particularly in rising interest rate scenario. To be placed in respective time buckets as per the next exercise date.
4. Deposits	
(a) Term deposits from public	
(i) Fixed rate	Sensitive could reprice on maturity or in case of premature withdrawal being permitted, after the lock-in period, if any, stipulated for such withdrawal. To be slotted in respective time buckets as per residual maturity or as per residual lock-in period, as the case may be. The prematurely withdrawable deposits with no lock-in period or past such lock-in period should be slotted in the earliest/shortest time bucket.
(ii) Floating rate	Sensitive reprice on the contractual rollover date. To be slotted in the respective time buckets as per the next repricing date.
(b) Certificates of deposits and ICDs	Sensitive reprice on maturity. To be slotted as per the residual maturity in the respective time buckets.
5. Borrowings	
(a) Term money borrowing	Sensitive reprices on maturity. To be placed as per residual maturity in the relative time bucket.
(b) Borrowings from RBI, Govt. and others:	
(i) Fixed rate	Sensitive reprice on maturity. To be placed as per residual maturity in the relative time bucket. Sensitive; reprice on the rollover/ repricing date.

(ii) Floating rate	To be placed as per residual period to the repricing date in the relative time bucket
6. Current Liabilities and Provisions: (a) Sundry creditors (b) Expenses payable (c) Swap Adjustment A/c (d) Advance income received/receipts from borrowers pending adjustment (e) Interest payable on (f) Bonds/deposits (g) Provisions	Non-sensitive.
7. Repos/bills rediscounted/forex swaps (Sell/Buy)	Sensitive reprice on maturity. To be placed as per residual period to the repricing bucket.
Assets	
1. Cash (incl. remittance in transit)	Non-sensitive.
2. Balance with RBI	Non-sensitive (since only current account is maintained with RBI).
3. Balances with other banks in India (a) In Current A/c (b) In deposit accounts, money at call and short notice and other placements	 Non-sensitive. Sensitive reprices on maturity. To be placed as per residual maturity in respective time buckets.
4. Investments (a) Fixed income securities (e.g., Government securities, zero coupon bonds, debentures, cumulative,. non-cumulative, redeemable preference shares, etc.) (b) Floating rate securities (c) Equity shares, convertible preference shares, shares of subsidiaries/joint ventures, Venture capital units	 Sensitive on maturity. To be slotted as per residual maturity. However, the bonds/debentures valued by applying NPA norms due to non-servicing of interest, should be shown. Net of provisions made in: (i) 3-5 year bucket – if substandard norms applied. (ii) 5-7 year bucket – if doubtful norms applied. Sensitive reprice on the next repricing date. To be slotted as per residual time to the repricing date. Non-sensitive.
5. Advance (Performing) (a) Bills of exchange, promissory notes discounted and rediscounted (b) Term loans/corporate loans/short-term loans (rupee loans only)	 Sensitive on maturity. To be slotted as per the residual usance of the underlying bills. Sensitive on cash flow/maturity.

(i) Fixed rate	Sensitive only when PLR or risk premium is changed by the FIs.
(ii) Floating rate	The amount of term loans should be slotted in time buckets which correspond to the time taken by FIs to effect changes in their PLR in response to market interest rates.
6. Non-performing Loans (Net of provisions, interest suspense and claims received from ECGC) (a) Substandard (b) Doubtful and loss	To be slotted as indicated at item B.7 of Appendix 1.
7. Assets on lease	The cash flows on lease assets are sensitive to changes in interest rates. The leased asset cash flows be slotted in the time buckets as per timing of the cash flows.
8. Fixed assets (excluding assets on lease)	Non-sensitive.
9. Other assets	
10. Repos/bills rediscounted/forex swaps (Sell/Buy)	Sensitive reprices on maturity. To be placed as per residual maturity in respective time buckets.
Assets	
1. Cash (incl. Remittance in transit)	Non-sensitive
2. Balance with RBI	Non-sensitive (since only current account is maintained with RBI).
3. Balance with other banks in India (a) In Current A/c (b) In deposit account, money at call and short notice and other placements.	Non-sensitive. Sensitive on maturity. To be slotted as per residual maturity.
4. Investments (a) Fixed income securities (e.g., Government securities, zero coupon bonds, debenture, cumulative, non-cumulative. redeemable preference shares. etc.)	Sensitive on maturity. To be slotted as per residual maturity. However, the bonds/debentures valued by applying NPA norms due to non-servicing of interest, should be shown, net of provisions made.

❋ ❋ ❋